SWIFT VICTORY

SWIFT VICTORY

*The Gifts of the
Holy Spirit at Work
in Your Soul*

by Walter Farrell, O.P.
and Dominic Hughes, O.P.

Roman Catholic Books
A Division of Catholic Media Apostolate, Harrison, New York
Business office: Post Office Box 2286, Fort Collins, CO 80522

Nihil Obstat
>>Thomas J. McHugh, LL.D.
>>*Censor*

Imprimatur
>>✠ Jerome D. Hannan
>>*Bishop of Scranton*

Scranton, June 16, 1955

ISBN 0-912141-49-2

Contents

I	"Sanctify Them in Truth": Grace and the Gifts	1
II	"Children of the Light": The Gift of Understanding	27
III	"More Beautiful than They": The Gift of Knowledge	53
IV	"The Seal of Resemblance": The Gift of Wisdom	79
V	"Let It Be So Now": The Gift of Counsel	105
VI	Family Likeness: The Gift of Piety	129
VII	The Poor and Their Fears: The Gift of Fear	155
VIII	Tranquil Violence: The Gift of Fortitude	173
IX	Swift Victory: The Gifts for Glory	195

PUBLISHER'S NOTE

Chapters I through V and Chapter IX are by Fr. Hughes; Chapters VI through VIII are by Fr. Farrell.

I
"Sanctify Them in Truth"
Grace and the Gifts

"Sanctify Them in Truth"

In an "age of anxiety" everyone needs assurances. When the cynicism of a few steals the certitude of almost all, ageless longings of the human mind and heart become especially acute. Men worry so much about relatively infinitesimal details that they cannot wonder at the Infinite. They are clinging so desperately to a mere foothold in intellectual security that they cannot enjoy the view from the cliff-edge of mystery. Refusing the help of the revealing Word, most men grope along searching for something of which they can be sure either within their own hearts or in the world around them.

Those who are sure that if men can control their environment they can resolve their inner conflicts still have in their bones the confidence of Bacon's dictum that science is power. In their blood flows Comte's messianism that to know is to predict and to provide. That providence demands a mass of statistics, since to be certain of anything they must know everything. The more men know, the more they need to know, not only for intellectual security but for physical survival. They search deeper within the ways of nature to find a way out; yet they become more entangled in a morass of matter, shifting circumstances, and details they are incapable of interpreting. Although they are looking for stability and purity, which are the fundamentals of sanctity, they are searching for them where they cannot be found and in a spirit of independence which refuses to accept what is not the product of human ingenuity through the physical, biological, and sociological sciences. They would rather walk in a widening circle of insecurity than ask the way.

No less anxious for assurance are those who seek certitude, not from the world around but from an introspective, intuitive experience. Many of them have traveled with Shaw and Wells the dreary cycle of theories from "all will be well" through "all must be made better" to "no good can come of this." They have unlearned through disillusionment what they had learned in sophistication. They are suspicious of scientific prophecies which have engineered men into a position for self-destruction without educating them in a philosophy of survival. For a few there may be an artificial *élan* in the arts—a moment of seemingly contactual sensation with something spiritual. For them this is their expected measure of immortality. Most who seek for security within themselves have no better solace than the feeling "This may be a poor way to live, but it is my own—and only." The living moment is an inner experience, and for many it alone is real.

These apparently opposing views have a common cord. Nature is their norm and man their end. Human life is self-contained and self-conclusive. Even if an Architect or Absolute is admitted as the origin of all that exists, that same Absolute is not accepted as the end toward which all tends. From this denial of a recognizable and realizable finality for life arises the fundamental neurosis of the age of anxiety. Men grow old in a search for security within themselves or in the world around, but they never reach the maturity of judgment to recognize that what they seek cannot be grasped by nature but must be given by God. Nor do they attain that independence of their own prejudices which frees them to accept first as a possibility, then as a reality, supernatural adoption and eternal security from their heavenly Father.

Although children who have an All-Wise and Loving Father are not burdened with the solicitudes and anxieties of their contemporaries, they cannot fail to appreciate similar intellectual and emotional tensions. Their living Faith leaves no place for misgivings about the facts of supernatural life, but their awareness of their weakness and unworthiness makes fear and trembling an ever-present reality, "for the thoughts of mortal men are fearful, and our counsels uncertain" (Wis. 9, 14). In order to fulfill the will of God, they too want the reassurance of objective answers and inward experience. They appreciate the problems of others because they understand themselves as they are and as they might be without grace. Whatever is normal in human longing, they feel more intensely because of their greater love; and wherever men search for answers, they look for analogies to illustrate supernatural mysteries. From the very beginning of their search they recognize their dependence upon God for ultimate enlightenment, from the initiation of Faith to the intuition of the Divine Essence in eternal glory. They are aware, too, of another subordination, their reliance upon the merits, satisfaction, and intercession of Christ. In Him they have known the Master of Truth, and from Him they have, as has their heavenly Father, a precise and poignant expression of both human longing and the Divine Will in Christ's priestly prayer: "Sanctify them in truth" (John 17, 17).

In that petition human longing is summarized and supernaturalized. In it men can find an intimate expression of the entire economy of salvation. For Christ, as the High Priest of all, first uttered the prayer at the solemn hour when He had concluded His sacramental sacrifice at the Last Supper and immediately before His bloody Passion. The same priest forever, He continues now "always living to make intercession for us" (Heb. 7, 25). He asked for what He knew would take place, yet He knew that it would take place because He asked. This was His hour of sacrifice for the salvation of men. He had docilely petitioned His heavenly Father: "Glorify thy Son, that thy Son may glorify thee" (John 17, 1), and He would confidently add: "Father, I will that where I am, they also whom thou hast given me may be with me; that they may see my glory, which thou hast given me" (John 17, 24). In the midst of His long and enlightening discourse He placed two other petitions, describing not the beginning and ending of the salvation of men, but the space of life between.

In Christian life on earth there are two correlative elements: a preservation from evil and a perfection in good. For both of these Christ prayed. "Holy Father, keep them in thy name whom thou hast given me" (John 17, 11) is the realistic request of one who knows what is in man. He did not "pray that thou shouldst take them out of the world, but that thou shouldst keep them from evil" (John 17, 16), since He knew that the engrafted evil of original sin left its mark upon all in their inclination to evil in proud self-assertiveness and sensual satisfaction. If, therefore, those whom the Father has chosen to be "holy and without blemish in his sight in love" were to continue to be not unworthy to be adopted through Jesus Christ as His sons, according to the purpose of His will, "unto the praise of the glory of his grace" (Ephes. 1, 4-5), divine power must sequester them from evil. Yet a negative protection from environment is not the essence of even earthly Christian life. There is a positive, perfective element, an inward experience of the ultimate reality for which Christ prayed in the most cogent and consoling of petitions: "Sanctify them in truth" (John 17, 17).

Send them the Holy Spirit is, according to St. John Chrysostom, (Homily 81) the concrete request contained in Christ's simple petition. In His Person and by His presence souls experience sanctity in truth and conformity to Christ. He is the "Spirit of truth, who proceedeth from the Father" (John 15, 26) and "testifieth that Christ is the truth" (1 John 5, 6). His presence among men is integral to the redemptive mission of Christ, who said ". . . the Advocate, the Holy Spirit, whom the Father will send in my name, he will teach you all things, and bring to your mind whatever I have said to you" (John 14, 26).[1] To accept and to appreciate in its fullest significance the "word of reconciliation" (2 Cor. 5, 19)—in fact, to be saved by the interior and invisible presence of the grace of Christ—each person needs the Holy Spirit. Every human longing for objective answers and inward experience is superabundantly fulfilled by His presence in the essence of the soul and His Gifts in its powers, as well as by His preservation of truth in Sacred Scripture and the tradition of Christ's Church.

The guardianship of the Holy Spirit over the sacred mysteries of faith is fundamental to the fulfillment of Christ's prayer "Sanctify them in truth." The Holy Spirit has as His special office the preservation of supernatural mysteries in their pristine integrity and inner harmony, allowing no point of doctrine to be exaggerated or minimized in the true Church. At the same time that He preserves intact and without increase the deposit of faith transmitted to the faithful, He inspires a constant development of the faithful in the faith. From Him comes every understanding, since "the Spirit searches all things, even the deep things of God" (1 Cor. 2, 10), and God "has revealed them through his Spirit" (Ibid.). Within the scope of His inspiration is every effort of the human mind to search soberly, piously, and sedulously the divine mysteries and to reach a fruitful understanding of them. He suggests the analogies which are apt in linking natural knowledge with supernatural revelation; He offers interior inspirations to explain the contrasts and connections among the mysteries of God, of grace and of glory. In a concrete and practical way He enlightens souls in the relationship of the mysteries of grace to their ultimate supernatural end, since "whosoever are led by the Spirit of God, they are the sons of God . . . and if sons, heirs

---

[1] From *The New Testament* as revised by the Confraternity of Christian Doctrine (St. Anthony Guild Press, 1941). Modern English renderings elsewhere in this book are from this edition.

also; heirs indeed of God, and joint heirs with Christ" (Rom. 8, 14ff.).

Among the most dynamic and dramatic mysteries of grace which the Holy Spirit gradually unfolds to souls is the fact and the significance of His own presence within them. When "the Spirit himself giveth testimony to our spirit, that we are the sons of God" (Rom. 8, 16), He certifies His own presence within the souls of the faithful. Through Him, moreover, souls are aware of the indwelling of the Triune God, since "in this we know that he abideth in us, by the Spirit which he hath given us" (1 John 3, 24). His making His presence known to souls is, moreover, a fulfillment of the promise of Christ: "I will ask the Father, and he shall give you another Paraclete, that he may abide with you for ever, the spirit of truth, whom the world cannot receive, because it seeth him not, nor knoweth him: but you shall know him, because he shall abide with you, and shall be in you" (John 14, 16ff.).

The Holy Spirit dwells in souls, not only to honor them and adorn them, but to influence their powers and actions. He crowns the work of every virtue, "because the charity of God is poured forth in our hearts, by the Holy Spirit who has been given to us" (Rom. 5, 5). He grants, moreover, that those in whose souls he dwells may live in friendship with God in conformity with Christ, "being transformed into his very image from glory to glory, as through the Spirit of the Lord" (2 Cor. 3, 18). From the same Spirit comes the grace to live, not only virtuously after a human fashion, but even divinely, according to the norms and measure of the Holy Spirit Himself. The experience of these inspirations, for which tradition has reserved the special name "Gifts of the Holy Spirit," is the climax of Christian life and the completion in souls of Christ's priestly prayer: "Sanctify them in truth" (John 17, 17). A lesser blessing by far than actual experience, but by no means negligible in the grace-to-grace process of sanctification in truth, is a supernaturally based and humanly elaborated understanding—inspired perhaps by the same Holy Spirit—of the existence, nature, and internal ordering of His Gifts.

The existence of these precious Gifts of the Holy Spirit is an integral part of supernatural revelation. Natural observation may give evidence of resultant phenomena, but of the cause of acts of the Gifts the human mind without the aid of Faith is ignorant. To natural judgment actions which come from these fixed principles of divine living are complexes, religious neuroses. Or, more simply, men might say of those who so act what was said of the Apostles at Pentecost: "These men are full of new wine" (Acts 2, 13). Nature has no norms, since "the sensual man perceiveth not these things that are of the Spirit of God, for it is foolishness to him, and he cannot understand, because it is spiritually examined" (1 Cor. 2, 15). The spiritual man, however, "judgeth all things, and he himself is judged of no man" (Ibid.). He reads Sacred Scripture with an eye enlightened by Faith, and he meditates fruitfully upon the full significance of what his Faith presents.

The revelation of the existence of the Gifts of the Holy Spirit involves one of the most intimate and intricate relationships outside that of the Trinity itself. Basic to the entire doctrine of the Gifts of the Holy Spirit is the prophetic description of Isaias concerning the subordination of the Humanity of Christ to the Holy Spirit. The prophet foretold that Christ would receive the indwelling Spirit and His Gifts: ". . . the spirit of the Lord shall rest upon him: the spirit of wisdom, and of understanding, the spirit of counsel, and of fortitude, the spirit of knowledge, and of piety. And he shall be filled with the spirit of the fear of the Lord" (Isaias 11, 2ff.). The Holy Spirit, therefore, is as much—and indeed far more—a part of the interior life of Christ, and a principle whereby Christ is "full of grace and truth" (John 1, 14), as that same Spirit is ever present in the visible mission of Christ.

From beginning to end of that visible mission, the Holy Spirit had a dominant role. He formed the body of Christ in the immaculate womb of the Virgin Mother, and He formulated in the minds of Elizabeth, Anna, and Simeon the first human testimony to the Savior (cf. Luke 1, 35-68; 2, 25). He descended visibly at Christ's baptism (Matt. 3, 16), and led Him into the desert to prove His Humanity and prepare for His apostolate (Luke 4, 1). Christ worked miracles "by the Spirit of God" (Matt. 12, 28), and He merited as priest-victim on the Cross when He "through the Holy Spirit offered himself unblemished unto God" (Heb. 9, 14).

Less obvious, but no less certain, are the interior inspirations of the Holy Spirit to which the human intellect and will of Christ were ever docile. That docility, moreover, was based not upon occasional stimuli but upon fixed principles within the soul of Christ. According to the prophet, the Holy Spirit would "rest upon him," abiding in Him and enabling even the perfect human powers of Christ to act in a divine way. The Holy Spirit imparted His Gifts so that the human nature of Christ might partake in every possible way in Divine Life, becoming the fullest participation of Divine Truth and Life and thereby most perfectly the Way. Through these Gifts the soul of Christ experienced the most complete submission to the Divine Will and the most perfect liberty of action. In these Gifts the Holy Spirit Himself accepted, and indeed absorbed, the powers of Christ's soul by filling them with grace and truth.

The plenitude of personal grace in the soul of Christ is in fact identical with His grace as Head of the mystical body. As He is, so He acts, "and of his fullness we have all received, grace for grace" (John 1, 16). In degree Christ's grace is infinitely exalted above that of any or all the members of the mystical body, but it is not essentially different. The human soul of Christ is endowed with an unrestricted share of Divine Life, but it remains human and is not divine. His human well-springs of activity approach divine knowing and loving, but they are not equal to them. In Christ, as in His coheirs, grace is a sharing of a life that is perfect only in the Deity. That share of the Divine Life includes not only a state pleasing to the Father but an intimate relationship especially appropriate to the Holy Spirit, a docility to His movements. This docility the human soul of Christ has in its integrity, and His followers in various inferior degrees. Yet there is an identity in the grace in Christ and in those conformed to Him, and consequently the prophetic description of Isaias has traditionally been understood and universally taught in the Church as applicable primarily to Christ and secondarily to each Christian.

Although the existence of the Gifts of the Holy Spirit in the faithful who are conformed to Christ is not a solemnly declared dogma, it is a part of tradition to which liturgical usage and the ordinary teaching authority of the Church give ample witness. For those who "perceive the things that are of the Spirit of God" (1 Cor. 2, 15) even a theoretical elaboration of this teaching may have its advantages. Only the Holy Spirit Himself makes the actual donation of these Gifts, but a human author may contribute to an awareness and prayerful desire for these graces which, to those properly disposed, God wisely and lovingly grants.

These "impartings of the Holy Spirit" (Heb. 2, 4) are unintelligible outside the context of the life of grace—the Living God in the lives of men. Those "born of God" (John 1, 13) by grace are as much like their Father as the differential of the Infinite and finite will allow. In the human frame of reference in which men theologically conceive the Living God, they distinguish what He is, what He has, and what He does—His Nature, His powers, His acts. Although in Him all three are utterly simple and undivided, in divine life as shared through grace these three are distinct realities. By grace, in the essence of their souls, men are first "made new"— "a new creature" (2 Cor. 5, 17); they are, in fact, made "consorts of the divine nature" (2 Peter 1, 4). They have, moreover, by the same divine gratuity, new supernatural powers to know and love God as their friend and ultimate reward, since in them "abide faith, hope and charity" (1 Cor. 13, 13). They have as well the infused moral virtues to act in human affairs from strictly supernatural motives. In each of their supernatural acts, too, there is the stimulus of grace, an actual sharing of divine life from moment to moment.

The Gifts of the Holy Spirit have their place in the lives of those "born of God," not as what makes them what they are, nor as what they do, but as something they have. The Gifts do not constitute divine life in the souls of men, nor are these Gifts merely passing actions, however meritorious. They are, rather, fixed principles of such acts, perfections of the powers of the soul itself. As something halfway between a power and an act, however, they are intelligible only in terms of their origin and their effect. They are habits—clothing the soul that it might act well.

Because the Gifts of the Holy Spirit are habits derived from sanctifying grace in the soul, they are clearly distinguished from those casual encounters of souls with the Holy Spirit called "gratuitous graces." These latter graces do not unite souls to God nor conform them to Christ, whatever marvels they may manifest. They are the "manifestation of the Spirit ... given ... for profit" (1 Cor. 12, 7), not to justify those who have them but that they may co-operate in the justification of others. With them the life of God passes through the soul, but nothing remains as evidence of an enduring, indwelling relationship. They have no necessary relationship to personal morals, but are rather of forensic advantage in the Church of God. By them some are able to have knowledge advantageous to others, to confirm that knowledge by convincing proofs, and to offer their knowledge in a way apt to interest their hearers. Prophecy, miracles, and the gift of tongues are of this category of graces, wherein the possessor is like a Prime Minister who has struck upon a formula for action without being any happier thereby. These extraordinary and sometimes startling graces are acts rather than habits. In them the Holy Spirit merely uses a man as His instrument for the salvation of others, as He did Caiphas prophesying quite accurately and unwittingly that it was better for Christ to die for the people. According to the needs and circumstances of the Church of God, therefore, the Holy Spirit employs these "ministries" and "workings," but on the other hand He unceasingly inspires—"rests upon"—souls with those habitual graces called His Gifts.

The Gifts of the Holy Spirit are habits in a strict supernatural application of that notion, according to the explicit testimony of the Fathers of the Church and of St. Thomas. The Gifts have, therefore, all the perfections and limitations of other habits and are best understood in terms of the common philosophical teaching on the nature of habits. For those accustomed to judge everything in terms of mass and multiplication the notion of quality and intensity, to which habits belong, is nebulous, if not negligible. Habits are modifications of the powers of the soul, perfecting them in their proper activity.

A knowledge of the proper activity of the various powers of the soul is basic to an understanding of habits, and consequently of the Gifts, since the grace of God perfects nature rather than destroys it. Because the soul is united to a body, its first awareness of reality is from the senses. Men, therefore, have sensory cognition and inclinations to sense goods through a "pleasure principle" (concupiscible appetite), and a desire for dominance (irascible appetite). Because the soul is in itself spiritual, it can transcend particularized experiences of the senses and have as its own the forms of other things. It does so by its power of intellect. When, moreover, the intellect presents a reality as attractive, an intellectual appetite, the will, is inclined toward that reality as a good. By their constant interaction the spiritual powers of the soul, the intellect and will, control and condition the basic humanness of life.

This human control of actions is a unique prerogative but not an absolute perfection. Men are superior to the brutes in what they can do, but inferior to the angels in the way they do it. Men's ability to deliberate is to their credit; their need to deliberate is a liability. If men are not limited to instincts and impulses, they are limited to creeping toward a conclusion an angel would know at a glance. In speculative matters, man's reasoning forces him to know various ideas and judgments separately and successively. In two distinct acts he first understands the premises of an argument, and those premises cause his knowledge of the conclusion. He knows one thing from another. In divine understanding, however, the intellect knows one thing in another, and it conceives the conclusion within the premise in a single, simple act. In this case, the premise does not cause the conclusion, although God knows in a single judgment that the content of the premise causes the conclusion. Any student moving from page to page in his textbook knows successively the arguments and the conclusions of the author, and his own knowledge is dependent upon the pattern; an instructor, on the other hand, may have the conclusions from another source, and not from the author's arguments, but at the same time see that the arguments do cause the author's conclusion, which is identical with his own. In practical matters involving the will, the progress is the same. A man knows and wills an end, as he had formulated an argument, and subsequently he chooses means, as he had reached a speculative conclusion. To choose the most appropriate means he must take counsel concerning the various possibilities. Through a process of trial he comes to know what is best in the ordinary or extraordinary situations in which he finds himself. Yet this procedure is painfully slow, and even when he has made his choice he must forcefully order it into act by commanding its execution amid changing circumstances. In the divine mode of willing, however, God does not first will an end and then, motivated by that, will various means. In an eternally simple act He wills both end and means—and these latter precisely as ordered to the end. In this way, God knows intuitively and wills instantaneously all things that have been, are, or will be. Although, therefore, both the divine and human intellects are, in broadest aspect, the ability to know, they are divergent in their manner of knowing or proper activity. It is the work of grace, and consequently of the Gifts of the Holy Spirit, to bring God's ways into human works through fixed principles of action.

The need for such fixed principles as the habits of grace in the powers of the soul is based upon a realistic and practical observation. Without abandoning for a moment an objective norm of morality or adopting the current "refer-it-to-the-biologist" attitude of popularized Freudianism, human reason can recognize, even—or especially—in a Christian context, Aristotle's fundamental moral principle *as a man is, so his end seems to him*. A proportion or balance must be realized between what is proposed and to whom it is proposed. His subjective disposition will not alter the end itself, but it will change his appreciation of it. He may hear and not perceive, see and not understand, even the most simple of sublime truths. If his fixed frame of mind is carnal, the more sublime the truth the more ridiculous it seems. Even if he has conscientiously and consistently practised purely natural good acts, his acquired virtue will not have directly prepared him for supernatural enlightenment and motivation. An interior teaching is necessary to elevate his mind to be supernatural so that it may see supernaturally, and to enable his will to love above all the Author of grace and the End of all merit. That interior preparation which proportions the soul to supernatural living, giving it a second nature like the divine and making divine actions connatural to human powers, is the entire economy of infused habits, both virtues and Gifts.

The fundamentals of human participation in divine activity are the infused virtues. By divine grant—and not otherwise—they come to exist in the soul, and to a divine end they are all ordered. Some attain that end directly, proportioning the powers of the soul to perceive something of God Himself. The primary participation in divine activity is to know something of God as He knows Himself by accepting His revelation in supernatural Faith. Confiding in His power and promises, the will already has something of eternal enjoyment in supernatural Hope. In Charity the direct relationship with God is consummated. Through it the will and the entire person are united with the Supreme Good; and all subordinate powers, habits, and acts are absorbed in a single bond of perfection. For the integrity of supernatural action, however, other virtues are required, regulating the means for fulfilling the obligations of Christian life and for removing the obstacles to their fulfillment. These are the infused moral virtues. Prudence enables the practical intelligence to distinguish good from evil in a supernatural ordering of means. Justice establishes the will in the fixed purpose of giving each and all his due upon the basis of supernatural judgment. Fortitude and Temperance, like their natural counterparts, give a participation of reasonableness to the irrational appetites, but according to norms unknown to a purely natural outlook.

In the activity of all these virtues, however, the natural powers of the soul have an important part. The object of the activity is no longer human but supernatural, yet the manner of acting is as before. In each act of virtue the human mind deliberates, chooses, and commands. The soul retains control over its powers; it can use them when it wills. In order to perform any of these actions, from the assent of Faith to the endurance of hardship, the soul must deliberate and decide. The actual grace of God must move to every act, but the soul, too, must move itself. From premise to conclusion, from the authority of God to assent to mystery, or from end to means, from the love of God above all to the fulfilling of His commandments in all, the soul is both moved and moves itself. For this a distinct condescension on the part of God is required. He allows souls to co-operate in the work of their own salvation, and yet the humanness involved in virtuous activity, a precious prerogative none would forswear, is a mark of imperfection. Although the powers of the intellect and will attain divine things by the virtues such as Faith and Charity, they do so in a human way, limping or lumbering along through a succession of interdependent acts. God tolerates this imperfect way of acting, even in man's highest supernatural acts, to show men how far they fall short of being perfect as their heavenly Father and how much they need Him. This very imperfection of human supernatural perfection, therefore, is the occasion and reason for an entirely new and different series of habitual graces from the Holy Spirit, His inspirations or Gifts.

The Gifts of the Holy Spirit differ intrinsically from the virtues; even from Faith, which sets the boundary of their activity, and Charity, which is the bond of their presence and perfection. They are dependent upon a different kind of grace moving them to act. In the practice of the virtues, the intellect and will, when moved by God's efficacious grace, move themselves to act by counsel, deliberation and decision. In the Gifts the activity is much more passive, more "... not I, but the grace of God with me" (1 Cor. 15, 10). The Holy Spirit operates in the soul in such a way that the soul has no need to move itself laboriously by deliberation and choice. The choice and command are already full-fashioned by the Holy Spirit, and the soul's activity is that of acceptance and assent. As in the first action of rational life, when God gives the soul its start in thinking, and in the justification of sinners when God raises the inert but not unresponsive soul to supernatural life, in every act of the Gifts of the Holy Spirit the motion is attributable not so much to the soul subordinate to God but to the Holy Spirit Himself supplementing human imperfections. In fact, the whole reason for the being and nature of the Gifts consists in a docility of human powers to the Holy Spirit, so that "the sons of God" may act in a divine way.

This ready mobility under the inspiration of the Holy Spirit is distinctive of the Gifts. All graces and virtuous actions are under His dominion. His Gifts, moreover, are distinctive as the final and perfective preparation of the human powers for docility to His inspiration. Because in the Gifts the soul does not move itself to act on the basis of some premise or previous decision, it is moved exclusively by a divine instinct. This impulse of divine love is not irrational, since the Holy Spirit never impels to action without at the same instant enlightening the soul. In every act of any of the Gifts there is both a sudden illumination and the swift surge of love. In Gifts whose character is predominantly intellectual, such as Knowledge or Counsel, illumination is more obvious, but affection is always present. In Gifts whose affective character is primary, the illumination of divine Counsel is never lacking. In all, the Holy Spirit unites in due measure science and sanctity, truth and love, a complete sanctification in truth. His movement, moreover, imparts certitude and security, since it has, not natural or human norms, but divine knowledge and action as its measure and rule.

The way in which the Gifts of the Holy Spirit share in the divine life as God lives it may be compared to the way in which the irrational part of man participates in reason through the moral virtues and prudence. The moral virtues of fortitude and temperance are resident, not in the will, but in the sense appetites themselves. By these virtues the pleasure-principle and the desire for dominance are so moderated that they readily respond to the command of prudence. Although there is nothing in the pleasure-principle itself to demand or suggest it, a chaste man immediately and instinctively resists temptations. His reaction is not attributable to any inclination of the sense appetite but to an impression left upon it by the practical judgments of prudence and commands of the will. In this way the pleasure-principle itself is intrinsically modified, and the irrational shares in reasonableness, the sensory in the spiritual. In parallel fashion, the deliberation of human reason is changed by divine intuition implanted in it by the Gifts, and the human way of acting is transformed by the divine. As Prudence forms the counsel, judgment, and command for the moral virtues, the Holy Spirit Himself provides the vision, certitude, and imperium for men to act divinely. Without invading human prerogatives, He takes to Himself human powers to a new manner of action. He supplies all preparatory judgments, all movement and direction; He orders and organizes all the factors necessary for divine actions in souls. He does all this by infusing His Gifts. In them He is not only the Mover of holy souls but their Master.

The Mastery of the Holy Spirit in the Gifts implies a further docility and passivity to His teaching, but it does not deprive souls of their co-efficiency of vitality, liberty, or merit. When the need to deliberate is taken away, an imperfection, not a prerogative, is removed. Under the inspiration of the Holy Spirit the soul acts as by instinct. Like the instinct of brutes, that of the Gifts gives evidence of a Higher Intelligence ordering acts to an end, but unlike that of brutes, the instinct of the spirit involves actual conscious submission. In that docility to what is higher, liberty is not only preserved—it is perfected. Liberty depends upon decision, not upon deliberation. Even if men ordinarily arrive at decision only through a long and laborious process of deliberation, such taking counsel and choosing are not essential to liberty as such. Divine liberty, at least, is exempt from that need. Although men see separately premises and conclusion, and will successively the end and the means, God acts more simply, and by contrast, instinctively, but not unwisely. In Him, and in souls who share His manner of acting through the Gifts, conclusions are not caused by previous judgments but contained within one judgment, and the means are self-evident in the willing of the end.

This manner of acting, normal for God, is something utterly new for men, even for the "sons of God." In it the heavenly Father's own perfection of knowing and loving is the measure and regulative principle, not merely the moving force. As God freely loves each particular good thing in the universe at the same time that He sees it in the context of All Good, Himself, so in its measure, the soul loves no particular good less than it should be loved but always within the scope of All Good. In this the soul is free. Moved by God, the soul actually experiences no other attraction, no other impulse, not even its own inertia; yet the real possibility remains for it to have done otherwise. No matter how closely associated with All Good a particular good may be, it is not identical with it, and toward that limited good the soul remains free. Any human action is a passing, particular thing, and as such the will is free to love it and will it or not, even when divine enlightenment gives evidence that such an act is the will of God. In this way the Virgin Mary was free at the Annunciation, although her "Be it done to me according to thy word" (Luke 1, 38) had been eternally determined as an expedient in the salvation of men. Likewise, the human will of Christ was free at the moment of His meritorious sacrifice on the Cross, although that redemptive act flowed from Christ's knowledge and obedience to an infallible divine decree. The object leaves them free, even if their act cannot be otherwise. Their very passivity to a higher rule of judgment liberates them from deliberation and for decision. Untrammelled by the network of its own acts, the soul inspired by the Holy Spirit forcefully and infallibly considers and chooses what God wills for it at that moment. It learns and it lives in a new and more perfect way, and yet it loses nothing of the perfection it had before through liberty and merit.

Although the soul acting under the Gifts is free and merits in each act, it has no dominion over these acts. It cannot summon the Holy Spirit when it wills, nor can it decide to perform an act of His Gifts whenever it chooses. Its exclusive function is to prepare itself for

His working, to remove, by His co-operating grace in the virtues, the obstacles to complete docility. The great mystics could not experience contemplation when they willed but only when it was given them by the infusion and inspiration of the Holy Spirit. Their ascetic lives removed obstacles, and their living Faith and intense Charity disposed them to receive the actual grace which would stimulate the Gifts into action.

As the foundation for friendship between God and the soul, Charity is a condition for the existence of the Gifts and makes a contribution to their activity. Since friends are as one in affection and "God is love, and he who abides in love abides in God, and God in him" (I John 4, 16), Charity is of the essence of every intimate union with God. This inherence or espousal of the soul with the Holy Spirit is the normal consequence of true love, in which the one loving is absorbed in the beloved, since one who loves has his end in the beloved and even is transformed into that goodness which attracts him. He is ardently passive, and thereby made perfect. In the case of the soul's relationship to the Gifts, this is especially true. The moving principle of the virtues is the Holy Spirit, but their immediate principle is the deliberation of reason. In the Gifts, not only the moving principle but the immediate formative and regulative principle is the Holy Spirit. He must be in the soul, if the soul is to live in Him, "because the charity of God is poured forth in our hearts by the Holy Spirit who has been given to us" (Rom. 5, 5). Love, as the Uncreated Third Person of the Trinity and as the inherent supernatural virtue, is not only the cause but the light of Knowledge. Love's blindness is sensual not spiritual, since a spiritual union enlightens by giving the soul contact with its Beloved. The more perfectly the soul is united to the Holy Spirit, the more likely too are the actual operations of the Gifts. The more closely united in friendship, the more intimately the soul and the Spirit share the secrets of love. Charity, then, is the subjective measure for the activity of the Gifts, although the Holy Spirit Himself is the objective and absolute norm for all things that transpire through His Gifts, since in every act divine love anticipates and causes Charity to rise and return to its source.

Charity, moreover, serves not only as the cohesive force uniting the soul with God, but it joins and orders the Gifts among themselves. Just as the various moral virtues do not go off on their own particular tangents but operate in co-ordination through the federating power of prudence, so the Gifts are connected through Charity. Prudence is the source of the practical reason of the choice and command by which the soul determines itself in various acts. In a parallel position, Charity is the unitive force which God uses to simplify the spiritual life and to bring a unity into the diversity of Gifts through which the soul may act in a divine way. That diversity, however, is not destroyed by the unifying force of Charity, but each of the Gifts remains distinct from every other Gift, virtue, and grace given to souls. That unity in diversity and diversity in unity is the mark of divinity, since God is no less provident in the order of grace than in the order of nature, and He has provided men with one soul and an assortment of powers.

To each of these powers something of the divine life is apportioned. None is too exalted to need it, none too lowly to receive it. The basic line of demarcation among the Gifts is the distinction of the powers themselves, and no Gift is in more than one power, no matter how many relationships it may have to various virtues, or several Gifts to one virtue.

In the intellect there are four Gifts. For that function of the intellect which has no other end than to observe or contemplate objects presented to it, there are three Gifts. The Gift of Understanding is a loving intellectual penetration by the "children of the light" of the darkness of the mysteries of Faith, which are the principles of all supernatural thought and activity. The Gift of Knowledge, likewise related to Faith, lovingly judges of the created causes of things and affirms that whatever may be the attractiveness of the natural or supernatural effects of God, He Himself is "more beautiful than they." In the observing, but by no means idle, function of the intellect, moreover, is the Gift of Wisdom, which is aligned with Charity in the will and by which the soul receives from God, who is both Truth and Love, a "seal of resemblance." In the operational or practical function of the intellect is the Gift of Counsel, corresponding (as closely, at least, as the sweep of an eagle corresponds to the struggles of a mole) to the virtue of prudence. By Counsel the intellect has a science to predict and provide. By participating in a knowledge of divine providence at its source, the soul with Counsel can serenely affirm of all the changes which fulfill God's changeless will: "Let it be so now."

In the appetitive powers there are three Gifts. In the intellectual appetite or the will is the Gift of Piety, by which the soul enjoys a family likeness and familiarity with God and readily accepts the just obligations which are consequent upon such a relationship. Even the sense appetites are not so lowly that they cannot receive within themselves something of divine life and a divine way of acting. In the desire for dominance, the irascible appetite, is the Gift of Fortitude by which the soul acts with tranquil violence to gain heaven by sweeping aside or struggling against all obstacles. Finally, in the pleasure-principle, the concupiscible appetite, is the Gift of Fear by which the spiritually poor and their fears come to rest upon the bosom of their heavenly Father, having eliminated intemperate affections and established every ground for hope. It permeates with a divine way of life the least of perfectible powers, and it brings the highest form of living to the lowest font of life.

From the highest to the least power of the human soul, the Gifts of the Holy Spirit are arranged in orderly sequence. Yet this is an order of human and objective intelligibility, not an order either of infusion or activity. All the Gifts are infused at once, either at Baptism or at the restoration of the state of grace through Penance, and all remain through eternity, so long as the soul's love of God continues. According to the love of God and the God of Love, however, these Gifts are brought into act. Since their acts are in the innermost reaches of the soul, outward manifestations in the lives of the saints are not infallible signs of their sequence even for an individual soul. The Holy Spirit Himself employs the various Gifts as He wills, and the soul is not able to calculate whence He comes or whither He goes. Yet it is sure that He has come to stimulate it to act and that He remains in His Gifts to keep the soul docile to His further inspirations.

When, through His Gifts, He becomes the Love of the human will and the reason of human reason, "the Spirit helps our weakness" (Rom. 8, 26). This assistance of infused Gifts is necessary for salvation, since the Gifts and Charity are inseparable, and the supernatural love of God above all things is an absolute requisite for entrance into the joys of the Lord. All men may have a suspicion that they cannot live well, even momentarily, unless they can live eternally, but Christians are sure that they cannot live eternally unless they are prepared to live divinely.

The very thought of the Gifts as not only something pleasant to have but something absolutely necessary is a humbling and yet edifying experience. As in the case of the first justification, by which souls are brought from spiritual death to life, and that gift of perseverance by which they make the transition from mortal to eternal life, so in the Gifts it is especially apparent that "it is God who worketh in you both to will and to accomplish according to his good will" (Phil. 2, 13). In the face of the facts of the supernatural life, the only practical activity for the soul is to accept and contemplate in love the overwhelming generosity of God, since "all the ways of the Lord are mercy and truth" (Psalm 34, 10). From that consideration one must necessarily conclude that the return of the soul to God, the whole of moral life, is more than a matter of diagnosing ills and prescribing ways to avoid evil and do good according to human prudence. It will become increasingly obvious that the Gifts of the Holy Spirit are as necessary a part of Christian revelation as the Ten Commandments, and knowledge of them as much a part of moral life as the knowledge of many devotional practices. The appeal of any exposition of the Gifts, moreover, is not that of an exhortation but of an explanation. The soul is aroused not to do something it considers beneficial but to realize that it has become a "new man, who according to God is created in justice and holiness of truth" (Ephes. 4, 24).

The "holiness of truth" which is especially apparent in the Gifts of the Holy Spirit is a truly edifying experience. By these Gifts the least of Christians is prepared for real and complete mystical experiences. Although Christians may be startled at the occasional and exceptional graces given to some, even pagans, they often fail to realize that they have within themselves the proximate principles of the most profound contemplation and mystical life. Yet the more they realize that the least degree of Charity is the greatest love and the slightest knowledge of supernatural truths is the most valuable of sciences, the more they are aware of how superabundantly God has fulfilled their longing for panoramic and particularized knowledge through an intuitive experience of truth in goodness. Even a halting theological explanation, based upon Faith and human reason, rather than on the actual "suffering of divine things" can be of value in their intellectual and moral lives. From it they may have some slight glimpse of how, by sending the Holy Spirit, the Advocate and Consoler, together with the supernatural assistance of His Gifts, the heavenly Father has fulfilled in their souls Christ's priestly prayer: "Sanctify them in truth" (John 17, 17).

II
"Children of the Light"
The Gift of Understanding

"Children of the Light"

Everyone by nature wants to know—or at least be "in the know." Diplomats and barbers have, of course, a professional standing to preserve. Rectory housekeepers and rulers of nations have likewise their official reasons. Yet even outside such officialdom there is a common need to know. Men live longer on the truth than on food and air, since without it they suffocate and starve out not earthly existence but eternal happiness.

Happiness in thinking seems like anything but a happy thought to those whose whole program of life is merely to exist. In their pragmatic associations, thinking involves sitting down, and a wanton waste of man-hours of productivity. For others an effort to grasp objective truth is an alien—undoubtedly subversive—act in the community of the subconscious to which every modern man by right belongs. Even those who consciously gather information for bantering in conversation or bartering in commerce confuse their curiosity, a second-natured inclination to be "in the know," with human nature's basic drive to know the truth. All those, however, who would not, in conversation, be "caught dead" with a thought would soon die interiorly without some sustenance from the truth.

If men are unlike other mammals and like one another more by their concepts than their countenances, they are like creatures from widely different worlds in what they know and how they know it. No planetary experiences could differ as widely as the natural and the supernatural, no walks of life could be more divergent than the human and divine ways of knowing. In natural knowledge men have an awareness of the things of nature and the nature of things, and finally come to know the Author of it all. In supernatural knowledge they know their Triune Father, from whom come all good things. Even among those who have the good news of revelation there are many differences. Some bow their minds to assent to the Word of Life but do not live by it; others live and love and labor in the deliberate, practised steps of the way of virtue. A favored few—a proportion from time to time extended—of the faithful not only have the Gifts as habits but experience the loving impulse of the Holy Spirit teaching them all things. These have a full family life with God, a companionship with the saints, and are most aptly called "children of the light."

The children born "not of the will of the flesh, nor of the will of man, but of God" (John 1, 13), have at once a naïvete and a penetration that are astonishing. They share in the eternally simple intuitive judgment of God, yet their knowledge is as nothing in comparison with the face-to-face vision of God which climaxes their perfection and perseverance. Even the functioning of the intellectual Gifts is graduated. Wisdom, Knowledge, Counsel, Understanding may work as one in any soul to form a single judgment. Yet at other times the Holy Spirit may divide them and apportion to each need the act of an appropriate Gift. Because of the various objects with which they are concerned, the Gifts may be arranged in a hierarchy, and their acts may be more clearly distinguished. In this gradation, Wisdom holds the highest place and Understanding the most fundamental. In the grammar school of the supernatural, Understanding is the first grade for those who have believed the light and are thereby "children of light" (John 12, 25).

The starting point of the soul's eternal education through the intellectual Gifts is not its first awakening to the supernatural. Much has gone before. The Gift of Understanding presupposes a living Faith in all supernatural revelation, a complete assent to the Word of God, and a love that rises to the Heavenly Father. Natural sciences and talents are not required for the working of the Holy

Spirit, nor are they obstacles to His action. The functioning of natural understanding, however, is parallel to that of the Gift. Whatever the natural habit of understanding does in natural knowing, the act of the Gift does, and abundantly, since God is more provident in the supernatural order than in the natural. Yet for earthbound minds which either lack the experience of the Gift or want to reflect upon that experience, the action of the Gift of Understanding is perhaps best appreciated in comparison and contrast with the natural habit of the same name.

The habit of understanding is in nature an interpreter for the entire process of knowing. It distinguishes, yet unites, particular factual information or impressions and the universal formulae or fundamental generalizations of all the sciences. It deals, in short, with those primary principles which are applicable to every particular experience. When a boy breaks a window or a nation breaks a treaty, Understanding may not be able to put a finger on the peculiar psychology that motivates the acts, but it is certain that for these phenomena there is a sufficient reason. Moreover, the principle that every effect has a cause is basic to fixing an electric switch or finding God. In all such cases the habit of understanding operates to provide the tools for the search.

Although the principles of understanding enter into every intelligent act, all intellectual life does not end with them. The mind has a long way to go to reach scientific conclusions and the order of wisdom. Yet no analysis or experimentation, no authority or sophistry, can set aside the primary principles provided by the all but native habit of understanding. Physicists and psychiatrists, plumbers and planters, are each and all operating on the fundamental assumptions that agents have ends and effects have causes. They may search long for the libido of the atom or the fissions of abnormal personality conflicts, or they may be simply seeking the source of a leak or the best way to plow a field. In any case, they begin with the primary principles of understanding, not perhaps speculatively expressed but at least practically applied. To check their findings or to correct an error, moreover, they have to return to their starting point, a simple intuition of the incontestable first principles of thought.

These principles of reason are so indispensable in the process of thought that many have thought of the habit of understanding as an inherited characteristic rather than a personal acquisition. It is, rather, both. The disposition to understand, to universalize experience, is characteristically human, but the degree of proficiency with which it is done is acquired by the efforts of each individual. Some have a very active understanding that penetrates at a glance each substance and situation; others have a passive appreciation of principles and their application, once these are patiently explained. Education is not an important factor in understanding, but enlightened awareness of reality is.

Upon the awareness and certitude that the natural habit of understanding provides, supernatural Faith can be built. Without understanding, the mind is not prepared for any activity involving Faith, since without that natural certitude which understanding affords, supernatural Faith would hesitate to elaborate upon its creed. With the habit of understanding rightly used and reflexively analyzed, the soul that lives by Faith is prepared to appreciate the supernatural parallel, the Gift which the Holy Spirit has given and named Understanding (cf. Isaias 2, 1).

In contrast to the natural habit, the supernatural Gift of Understanding is a noon light after a night's groping. Natural understanding is a blind, ineffectual desire to touch with human thoughts God as He is. In its search it touches upon every truth within its reach, yet in no one or all of them does it find more than the words written in nature's Braille: "Beyond lies God."

Beyond the anticipation or appreciation of natural understanding are the infinite frontiers of supernatural mystery. There the Gift begins. From grace to grace, from mystery to mystery, the Holy Spirit moves the soul from one penetration to a new prospect, from renewed enlightenment to revealing enticements. The horizons of Understanding are constantly expanding across the entire territory of the Faith. Yet the view of Understanding is always somewhat horizontal, always on the level of a simple intuition without the off-cosmic vantage point granted in the analytic judgment of Wisdom. Understanding is a penetration of the first principles of supernatural life—the Triune God who is the Cause of all, and the triumph of men in being united to Him. It includes the same material coverage as Faith, the Gift of Knowledge and the Gift of Wisdom, but it acts in a clearly distinguishable way. The Gift of understanding is like Faith in its supernatural objects, but in its divine rather than human way of acting it is a Gift rather than a virtue. Among the various Gifts, Understanding is more like Knowledge and Wisdom than any of the other Gifts, because it is intellectual, and among intellectual activities Understanding operates in a supernatural manner whose closest parallel is the natural habit of understanding.

Understanding as a Gift, moreover, has a bifocal vision. It is directed to supernatural principles and truths, but it also sees natural principles in a new perspective. The simplicity and unity of God, for example, which are a climax for the most profound natural penetration, are rudimentary to supernatural Understanding, based upon the revealed word of God. In either natural or supernatural truths, Understanding penetrates to the marrow of reality: the underlayers of appearances, causes pregnant with effects, effects bearing into unending generations the character of their causes, and under words, words, words—a meaning.

More than meets the eye is obvious to Understanding. In the natural habit the vital movement to penetrate the truth arises from the mind, but the mold of the concepts from the nature of things. While the world puts its best face forward and the senses of a man are bewitched or bewildered, the habit of understanding will not allow the mind to play the prodigal or roam and revel amid superficialities. With monkish diligence, understanding selects its specimens, cloisters its concepts, and chooses the principles that will be prelates to all later thought. It may not be able to formulate exact definitions of everything the senses find for it to look at, but in each it sees that no weight, size, color, act in time or space, or any other passing phenomenon, is the core of what may be related. These lie deeper; thereto understanding plunges.

For the supernatural Gift of Understanding the way is already well prepared. Faith goes far. Yet its limits are fixed by the nod of a head, an assent of the mind to truths that in this life cannot be seen. What can be seen, natural understanding knows full well. The Apostles knew by natural observation that the Man who spoke with authority in their midst had power to command Lazarus or the lake, or to save a paralytic or a Pharisee. From their Faith, however, they were certain that He did these things as one from God, indeed as One with God. When they did not see, they heard His Word and they assented. Their assent, and likewise that of all who follow Christ, is not, however, the end of all intellectual activity. It is not a stultifying abnegation of, but an absorbing stimulant toward, understanding, and ultimately vision. The roadway of human effort to understand the things of Faith is strewn with the split syllogisms of heresies and the abandoned opinions of theologians; yet the way is constantly being pushed forward through a jungle of possible explanations. Each of these efforts is of value in clarifying and corroborating the Faith for men, but none or all of them is equal to a single upsweep of soul by the Holy Spirit through the Gift of Understanding.

In the act of Understanding there is nothing new, but everything is renewed. Souls that knew Christ see Him once again. They have a Tabor vision of the Truth, even if they can only stammer "Lord, it is good for us to be here" (Matt. 17, 4). They need no prohibition to keep their thoughts to themselves, since they have seen the ineffable. The intimate, intuitive act of the Holy Spirit upon and with their souls cannot be explained, but only experienced. The experience of the Gift, however, does not go beyond the objects in the scope of supernatural Faith, and even if the act itself is personal, the area of its operation is the common heritage of all Christians.

From Faith, for example, a Christian knows that the Incarnation is not a fusion of natures but a union in a Person. To this he must assent, to preserve in his mind the integrity of the authority of God revealing; yet the Nicodemus in him nudges his mind to inquire "How can these things be done?" (John 3, 9). Understanding, whose answer is imitated in the labors of theology, gives at least a shadow of an explanation. Anyone who would ask how many people, rather than how many human natures, were at a party has an inkling of natural understanding's notion of personality, the basis of all supernatural penetration. Personality is ordinarily coincident with human nature; where one is, the other is never absent. Yet in the Incarnation the situation is unique, and Understanding knows why, even if it cannot explain fully how this can be. In Christ the perfect human nature has no personality of its own, none that is human like itself. The personality is not destroyed nor the nature lessened, but the whole of the nature is assumed by the Person of the Word of God—and is better for it. In its penetrative judgment Understanding is certain that His human nature is thereby made perfect, and of inexpressible dignity.

To anyone without Understanding, it might seem better if Christ's human nature stood on its own two feet of essence and existence by its own personality. They would fail to see that there is greater dignity in men's being elevated by someone higher than in remaining by themselves; they would also be ignorant of the fact that it is more blessed to receive a higher gift from above than to dole out lesser gifts to those below. Yet these same persons would seek the advantages of education to be raised up and to be received into, not the metaphysical, but the psychological personality of the teacher. They think they take something away from the school, while, in reality and for better or for worse, they are taken away from themselves, absorbed, assumed as it were, into the teaching of the school. Such judgments of Understanding seem to jog the mind a bit and throw it off balance, but they merely disturb its complacency, and do not cause it doubts. Cogently and concretely, Understanding penetrates the perfect communion of the human and divine natures in the Word Incarnate in its singular splendor and innumerable consequences.

Understanding perceives that if a Divine Person does not act in a human nature, the life of Christ is false and the lives of Christians futile. Yet since He does not cease to be One with the Father and the Holy Spirit to be one with men, He redeemed men and reminds them of their heavenly Father in His every human action. In the tears of Christ, Understanding sees the mercy of God; in the temple lash, His justice. In His fatigue at the Samaritan well and His dialectic on the drinking of heavenly waters of grace, there is for Understanding a witness to the intimacy of detail and infallibility of procedure in His providence. Throughout His life, from His infancy to His immolation, there is a sub-surface of truth that does not escape the observation of Understanding.

When not only the Divinity but even the Humanity of Christ lies hidden in the Blessed Sacrament, Faith does not doubt, nor does Understanding default. Without asking to place a hand in His side or a finger in the imprint of the nails, Understanding has a certitude that Christ, risen from the dead, is really present in the Sacrament of sacraments. Understanding is likewise aware that Christ is not present as in the upper room, but substantially and without any distinguishable bodily position. His arms are not outstretched, but His mercy is unrestrained. He is not a captive in the tabernacle, but rather He captivates the hearts of all who leave the imprisonment of their own selfishness long enough to share His happiness. In the Sacrifice of the Mass, Christ is not some prelate of past ceremonies but the principal priest who offers the holocaust of Himself to His heavenly Father. Nor is He passive in the act of Holy Communion; He absorbs the soul to Himself in a union of love which binds the soul to all who share in Him.

In Christ in His historic or Eucharistic presence the Gift of Understanding has its principal supernatural opportunity to penetrate the underlayers of appearances. Under the accidents of a human body, or merely bread, it attains to a substance, the Person of the Word or the presence of the Savior. Faith assents to the fact, but the loving intuition of Understanding has at least a glimpse of how these things can be, or at least cannot be otherwise. It more than scratches the surface, even if it does not quite comprehend the core of the mysteries of Faith. Little is left to conceal or confuse the true dimensions of the mysteries, and the "substance of things to be hoped for" is unearthed from mere appearances.

Besides dissecting the substance from its accidents, Understanding has the function of explaining the meaning of words. Chronicles of the chosen people or of the Beloved Son of God, prophecies and their fulfillment, words of wisdom or Wisdom's own, give up their inner meaning before its gaze. Each sacred text of truth, whose co-authors, divine and human, produced works like themselves, is simple yet significant, literal yet with latent connotations. A self-walled river, trumpet-toppled walls, or a sun that stands sentinel to a battle are facts of history, yet fathomless evidence of God's extraordinary care of His people, who were as often feckless as faithful. Of that care there is no end, and the events lose none of their reality in being symbols of the sacraments. People, too, are something more than themselves. Real as their lives were in bitterness or blessings, they represented something further. Abraham with his innumerable progeny and Melchisedech without known progenitors are more than men; they are symbolic anticipations of aspects of the priesthood of Christ. Moses in his leadership and legislation and David in his regal power and prayer are both historic figures and harbingers of One whose laws would be life-giving and whose kingdom would be heaven.

In words of wisdom, moreover, Understanding finds that her "conversation hath no bitterness, not her company any tediousness, but joy and gladness" (Wis. 8, 16). Understanding never tires in its search beneath the surface, and always rejoices in what it finds. For souls with Understanding the psalms are not antiquated poetry but prayers expressive of every human need. The other sapiential books are not anachronistic, pious musing, but meaningful and moving expressions of the will of God. In the prophets, Understanding need not have merely hindsight on what was once foreknowledge. Much of what is there written is timeless. With the words of Wisdom Himself, the Gift of Understanding has an unending preoccupation. His Sermon on the Mount, His prayer at the Last Supper, His brief discourses after His resurrection are summations of eternal truths for which Understanding delights to give an accounting. His enigmatic statements are accepted by Faith, but they are examined in Understanding. When Christ said "He that loveth his life shall lose it" (John 12, 25), he posed a problem for Understanding whose answer may lead to the avoidance of mortal sin, the entrance into a religious order, or the willing submission to martyrdom. In all His words the promised Paraclete inspires the soul to find a fuller, deeper meaning, the meaning the Holy Spirit Himself, as author of the sacred texts, intended them to convey. The significance of words of Sacred Scripture is, therefore, as much an object of the search of Understanding as the substance under accidents, or the causes behind effects.

In its intuition of the relationship of cause and effect, Understanding has perhaps its most subtle contact with reality. It taps a party line, knowing neither the sender nor the receiver of the communication thoroughly, but it has an intriguing awareness of a relationship between them. The language used in the conversation between God and creatures—or rather, the monologue to which the creature gives sporadic response—is not foreign to Understanding. It is the language of love. The Primal Love which gives glory to human beings and gates to Hell is, in Understanding's perception, the cause not only of effects, but of other subordinate causes in the cosmic strategies of His Providence. In this, Understanding finds the major evidence of the supremacy, the versatility, the ingenuity, and the gentleness of divine causality, since God not only accomplishes ends but allows men to contribute their efforts as secondary causes. In the eternal designs of God, the free actions of men have a part as great as—indeed greater than—the necessary movement of the celestial spheres. In those actions the delicacy of God's determinateness is most clearly evident, since each grace is measured by glory, and glory by God's holy Will. By Understanding, the soul is keenly aware that God does not love things because they are good, but by loving them makes them good, and by loving more makes them better. Yet God's loving Will toward creatures is inseparable from His Wisdom and His Providence. In that Providence, Understanding discerns pent-up possibilities and the cause of all that actually happens. More intelligently than most people read the newspaper, the soul with Understanding reads the headlines, hard facts, editorial explanations, even the comic passages in God's Providence. It goes beyond the assent of Faith to the righteous mercy and justice of God in preferring Jacob to Esau, and appreciates the legitimacy of countless repetitions of that same divine selective service for the militia of the kingdom of heaven. In willing good to some, God wills no moral evil to others; they fling themselves from His embrace with such violence that it takes them a whirling eternity to appreciate their loss. Yet God's Providence, and His subordinate but special predestination of the saints, remains a mystery to be penetrated, not a puzzle to be solved. The solution of the problem of Providence would mean the dissolution, in that mind, of the Cause of all effects which keep the soul in unending awe.

Of all the supernatural effects that Faith's mirror refracts to Understanding, none is more sublime than the "flesh" the Word assumed. In the act of uniting human nature to Himself, God wrought a marvel which would stimulate the minds of all the faithful and would be the occasion of a mere creature's most perfect act of Understanding. No more loving, devoted, virginal disposition of mind sequestered from all sensual imagining by Understanding is conceivable than that of the Blessed Virgin, about to be the Mother of God, and asking "How shall this be done, because I know not man?" When she asked, she had already conceived Christ in her soul by Faith. She likewise knew that the ordinary secondary cause in human generation was utterly incongruous if Emmanuel were to be her Son. Her question, unlike St. Paul's "Lord, what will you have me do?" (Acts 9, 6), is not a request for practical advice but a loving plea for contemplative enlightenment. A woman's curiosity, persistent and penetrative as it may be, cannot account for such a question. Rather, she who had already experienced many of the great things of Him Who is mighty asked, in the intimacy of love and under the inspiration of Love, "How?" The causal relationships in the Incarnation were not then, or ever, made completely comprehensible to a created intellect, but it was made quite clear to her and all men that in that generation none but the Triune God would be involved. The powerful Father and the sweet, forming Spirit would act within her, so that the Word might dwell with men, to redeem them from their sins and bring the world, full circle, back to the Cause of all good things, the provident Will of God.

Not every soul or every act of Understanding has so rewarding a reply. Yet in each there is a perception of the truth, a glimpse into the sanctuary of mystery. That darting penetration into mystery is the distinctive function of Understanding, its proper act, its whole reason for being. Its role in the supernatural life of the mind is not ornamental but functional, and its office is always related to, but never identified with, the functions of Faith and the light of glory at the two extremes of supernatural intellectual life, or the other intellectual Gifts in between. From each of these it is distinct by its unique act, yet with all it has much in common.

The truths with which Faith and Understanding are concerned are from the same book of revelation, often from the same page. Yet each has a different act, as widely separated in reaction to the witness of Faith as those of a wife and a trial attorney. The wife assents; the attorney, even to defend, inquires. The assent of Faith is not unenlightened or unintelligent, nor is it inquisitive and penetrating. Facts of supernatural life are taken on their face value because of the testimony of God revealing. Without the slightest hint of cynicism or doubt, Understanding adds a genuine but gentle critical approach. It questions not the light but its own limited vision. Where confusion is so easy and so tragic, when precision is so difficult and so rewarding, Understanding acts. It draws the line between the sensory and the spiritual, the natural and the supernatural, and everywhere it separates truth from error. It treads a narrow path. It knows that God has "hid these things from the wise and prudent," and has "revealed them to little ones" (Matt. 11, 25). It lovingly asks for enlightenment. With the speed and sureness of the Holy Spirit Himself, who moves the mind, Understanding takes the measure of metaphors, and in parables it grasps the essential point. With images—a shamrock or the soul's own powers to express the Trinity—it is both patient and ruthless. It uses them profusely, and then ushers them out with thanks for their provisional services. Understanding must be cautious in each step, because its vision is never complete.

The conclusive vision of total Trinitarian truth is beatific. The means of that vision is not Understanding alone, but the light of glory. With that light Faith is banished, and the soul need no longer strain to penetrate mysteries. Their meaning is visible at a glance. Understanding's function in heaven is not superfluous, and it is not absorbed into the act of vision. The vision is directed exclusively and completely toward God Himself; the act of Understanding is a loving reflection upon divine enjoyment, of which God is the source and the soul the beneficiary, the soul the vital principle and God the object. This bilateral reality, the conjunction in knowledge and love of the Infinite and the finite, will keep the soul ever in awe. The Holy Spirit Himself will eternally inspire the soul through Understanding to marvel at knowing God even as the soul itself is known by Him, and to magnify the Lord in unending canticles. Understanding, distinct from both, will continue its penetrative function with renewed perfection when Faith is no more and the light of glory will have freed the loving Christian from the "corruptible body" which "is a load upon the soul, and the earthly habitation" which "presseth down the mind" (Wisd. 9, 15).

While the mind is still pressed down by its earthly habitation it is helped to dwell with God through the Gifts of Knowledge and Wisdom, as well as through Understanding. From both of these Gifts Understanding is distinct. They are analytic in their judgment, but Understanding is not. Understanding forms a judgment, an affirmation or negation, but that judgment does not reduce a mystery to its component parts but has a penetrative apprehension of the whole. It satisfies the faithful, loving mind's first demand for evidence, but it does not give every accessible explanation. Such explanations come from the inspiration of the Holy Spirit through the Gifts of Knowledge or Wisdom, or through human effort in theology. Theology's syllogisms, although not hostile, are not the habitual mode of Understanding. They are fruit of labor. Understanding is the intuition of love. For the publication of an opinion the process of theological reasoning is more valuable than the intuition of Understanding, but the latter's concrete experience is of much greater cogency in personal conviction.

The personal conviction that arises from the act of the Gift of Understanding is perhaps its first effect upon the soul. While the very notion of assent in Faith implies a more ample knowledge in another who reveals, the notion of Understanding adds a personal touch to truth. Since objective truth and the subjective grasp of it are coefficients in the process of knowledge, unless the truth becomes a personal possession, it is lost. Exposure to truth is not experience, even in the supernatural order. Christ Himself promised His apostles a Paraclete who would teach them all things which Christ had revealed. Nothing halts a teacher sooner than a student's density or defiance in understanding, and nothing is more rewarding to both the teacher and the student than their mutual co-operation in the student's vital discovery of the truth. In supernatural truths this discovery does away as far as possible with the mere relationship of mind to mystery and makes it person to Person. Then the soul knows, as it were, no longer by the proxy of Faith, but by a personal, if distant, contact. In Understanding the soul has an experience something like that of the Samaritans. They had heard the testimony of the woman at the well and were convinced, but after they have had personal contact with Christ they would tell her, "We now believe, not for thy saying; for we ourselves have heard him, and know that this is indeed the Savior of the world" (John 4, 42). Likewise, in Understanding, belief remains, but the personal discovery is so forceful that the whole truth seems like an utterly new experience. As with a teacher's repeated lesson, nothing penetrates the soul, because the soul penetrates nothing, until a new light is given; then with eye-widening delight the mind discovers what it had known or assented to for so long. The human experience of discovering what is known already is quite common; men discover their own doorsteps, their wives, their own souls. The closer the object is, it seems, the more out-of-focus it can become. A stimulant is needed to call to attention what is accepted so readily. In the supernatural life the stimulant is Charity and the overshadowing Love of the Holy Spirit. The acceptance is the assent of Faith, and the discovery is the penetrating intuition of the act of Understanding.

The discovery of Understanding does not change the truth, but transfigures it. It is clothed in a new and luminous intelligibility, and the darkness of the surrounding concepts and images is in a more marked contrast. In this contrast is the almost automatic sloughing off of error. Just as human beings shed prejudices with personal contacts, the mind sheds the defilements of its own limited way of thinking because of the touch of truth. When, therefore, truth is made personal, it purifies.

Purity in the truth and from the truth is the second and more significant consequence of the act of the Gift of Understanding. It produces a "cleanliness of heart"—the only cleanliness truly approaching godliness. Such purity is not bodily restraint or emotional stability, nor even the virtues which control that cleanliness. It is something even higher. Before the act of Understanding can normally take place, the other purifying influences must have done their work. Through the virtue of temperance, gluttony—which results in grossness of mind and garrulousness, both enemies of Understanding—is eliminated. Through chastity, sensual desires that could, and did, destroy the wisdom of a Solomon are moderated or mortified. Yet these, and every other modification of unruly passions by the virtues, are presupposed to the final sweeping and garnishing of the soul by Understanding.

The "cleanliness of heart" produced through Understanding is the antiseptic of the spirit on the wound of the intellect already well washed by Faith. With a tingling certitude it frees the mind from the encrustations of errors and images, from its proneness to measure things by the human mind, and the mind by the senses. Antibodies harmful to the clear vision of the truth can no longer lurk in dark recesses of the mind; they are purged away in a process that is sometimes painful to those who have got used to living without light. Because of Understanding the human mind is a Magdalen, purified by the Holy Spirit, to see, even if not to touch, the Risen Christ. Before Understanding, the naked truth, like Truth Himself stripped of His garments, stands bare and unashamed. In Understanding, the mind is quickened to proceed without confusion and error, to discern the principles from the example, the mystery from the image. God need not have a long white beard, nor be represented by an eye. Nor is He, on the other hand, a vague abstraction, a formless spirit who floats about like fleecy clouds in the mind. He is a Person, knowing, loving, caring, chastising, comforting, purifying the minds of those who love Him so that He may prepare them for the happiness He has promised.

The happiness God has promised to the clean of heart is a vision of Himself: "Blessed are the clean of heart, for they shall see God" (Matt. 5, 8). There is no admission into heaven without the cleanliness of heart that Understanding provides. One may not have written books of mystical theology or had visions or ecstasies, but the laver of the Holy Spirit must have touched the soul, even at the time of the last anointing. Even before eleventh-hour, drastic purgations of the soul, however, there can be a true cleanliness of heart, and consequently the blessedness of seeing God. Just as God's mercy seems extravagant in the various ways it has devised to attract men to loving God, so His justice seems impetuous in its insistence upon an immediate reward for the work done, and done principally by the Holy Spirit Himself. Even in this life there is a reward of seeing God, not completely as in the beatific vision, but partially, yet more perfectly than ever before by that soul. Such souls with Understanding have a foretaste of what is to come. Fleetingly, imperfectly, they see God, because their hearts are pure and prepared. If fools do not see the same trees that wise men see, certainly the faithful who act in a human way through Faith, and even Charity, do not see supernatural mysteries in the same manner as those who are inspired to judge in a divine way by Understanding. They see because they are purified by Understanding, and by seeing are further purified to Understand more fully. Such is God's constant husbandry of souls. He prunes away preconceptions and prejudices with every new spring season of the soul. He provides, moreover, that each such passive yet willing acceptance of purgation is meritorious of the perfect and eternal vision of Himself. The soul with Understanding counts its own blessings better than anyone else. Because of its cleanliness of heart it is capable of appreciating that the supreme dominion is to be dependent upon God, the most sublime enlightenment is to be enveloped in mystery, the greatest personal liberty is to be purged of oneself. Through Understanding the soul is cleansed and sees God; and in that vision, even in this life, the soul is blessed.

The supreme acts of the beatitude of cleanliness of heart, which belong to the perfection of human and divine living, are not the only benefits that Understanding initiates in the soul. There is a more common and constant enjoyment of God called a fruit of the Holy Spirit. If the beatitude is the soaring pursuit of an infinitely elusive reality in mystery, the fruit is an awareness of an absorbing and abiding presence. The fruit that is consequent upon Understanding is the ninth of twelve fruits named by St. Paul (Gal. 5, 23), and called "faith." Although it is an entirely supernatural entity, it may be described in terms of its natural counterpart, which everyone knows from human life; from experience comes faith. The faith indicated by St. Paul as the fruit of the Holy Spirit is not the theological virtue which is an assent to divine authority that must precede any experience, but a confidence based upon the loving experience of truth. Such confidence is not the brash daring of youth, which relies only on itself, but the conviction that the soul can accomplish much more than it dared to imagine, if it is assisted, enlightened, and elevated by God.

Just as in the taking of medicines there is at first a conjecture and then a conviction, a reliance upon the authority of a doctor and druggist and then a personal experience of benefit, so in the supernatural life there is an opportunity for a divine experience which only a test can tell. From that experience which Understanding provides, there is no analysis of the precise causes of the renewed confidence in the soul, but there is an awareness that God is the cause and that the soul is blessed by the cleanliness of heart to see Him. A transfiguration in the mysteries as true as that on Tabor takes place within the soul, and it has an unshakable conviction that it has known and can know much more of the mysteries of supernatural life. The fruit of experience is final in any series of acts of Understanding, but it is not the finale in divine enjoyment. The soul says within itself: "I have sat in the shadow of him whom I desired, and his fruit is sweet to my mouth" (Cant. 2, 3), yet it realizes that the sweetness of the fruit is neither sentimentality nor self-satisfaction, nor anything complete in itself, since the soul has known only His shadow in Faith and still desires Him with the Hope of eternal possession. Yet the closeness of His presence is a rest of the soul, inspiring in it an abiding confidence in the guiding, kindly light of the Holy Spirit through the intensified darkness of the mysteries of Faith.

Mystery remains the orbit of Understanding. It dwells and even delights therein with a confident and consoling discontent. The mind with Understanding is somewhat like the manager of a modern motel, knowing all the roads and never on them. Understanding knows how far it is from the first assent of Faith and where lie Knowledge and Wisdom on the highway of the spirit, but it stays home with its primary principles and makes no excursions into analysis. Yet it has a hearth-side confidence in what it knows; it may not know all there is to be known even about its own country of first principles, but it is never lost. It lends a light, even if it cannot lead the way.

The light of Understanding, like that of Faith itself, is first of all to know the truth and secondly to do what is expected of it, under grace. In its very intuition of the truth, however, there is a practical significance, since the truths of God which cannot be altered are the reasons for the amendment of human lives. Conformity with its principles is demanded for the perfection of any creature, and especially of a human soul. A Triune God, in Understanding's keen perception, is the cause of all, and in Him all things end. Contemplating this truth, Understanding cannot fail to realize that this applies to every man, and that none is ever happy unless he has eternal life—"this is everlasting life, that they may know thee, the only true God, and Jesus Christ, whom thou hast sent" (John 17, 3). Nothing more practical can be given to men to know than that they have no merely natural end. With that knowledge all they do is different. They "mind the things that are above, not the things that are upon the earth" (Col. 3, 2).

In their search for things above, they are not less practical but more prayerful. They see in prayer a profound and powerful force for good. From Understanding and a cleanliness of heart they have a tantalizing experience of the truth, and in faith, the fruit of Understanding, they have a daring confidence. In this spirit they consider the rest of their lives as negligible, or as nothing at all. They are willing and eager to lose their lives that they may find them, to die to nothingness to gain everything. They pray "Thy kingdom come" (Matt. 6, 10). That stark, striking, searing petition cannot be restrained in a soul that understands. The whole of life is then a last advent hour, a hushed contemplative expectancy of the epiphany of Truth as Savior and as Judge. All the facts and formulae that have been painstakingly assembled in meditation and reading are summed up, simplified, and personalized for the soul whose clean heart is its clear judgment of the Truth. The clear judgment that seeks first the kingdom of heaven does not set aside all concern for things of the earth. The penetration of mysteries does not become the soul's only occupation, but it is definitely its preoccupation, its preferred delight, and a preparation for consummate joy.

During the long wait for the answer to its prayer that the kingdom of heaven would come, so that the soul might "enter into the joy of the Lord" (Matt. 25, 21), it is sustained by faith, the fruit of Understanding, and constantly purified by the movement of the Holy Spirit. Vocal prayers, or any prayers with a fixed formula, have not the ennui of routine but the energizing experience of something familiar but fathomless. The liturgical cycle of feasts will be as fascinating as the heavens are to an astronomer. Mass will be more than a Sacrifice between an oblation and a communion; it will be the daily forged link between Primal Love and perpetual happiness. In all the sacraments the negotiable securities of salvation will be more in evidence, and the commerce of grace will be intensified. Their souls "beholding the glory of the Lord with open face, are transformed into the same image from glory to glory, as by the Spirit of the Lord" (2 Cor. 3, 18).

To the image of God, from grace to grace, is a gradual growth. Its full maturity in this life is the function of Knowledge and Wisdom among the Gifts of the Holy Spirit. Its beginning belongs to

Understanding. That Gift is pedagogue to the soul, preparing it for Wisdom. Accepting the mysteries of Faith and never going beyond their scope, Understanding nonetheless probes and penetrates everywhere the substance under accident, the meaning under words, and the relationship of cause and effect. Impetuous and impertinent by the adult standards of virtues practised in a human way, it has a childlike inquisitiveness from the Holy Spirit of all inquiry. A privilege and a Gift, Understanding is at the same time the property of those who have believed the light and are thereby the "children of light" (John 12, 25).

Understanding
(*Summary from the* Summa)

"Understanding implies an intimate knowledge . . . a supernatural light to penetrate . . . that whatever may be the external appearances, they do not contradict the truth. . . . The Gift of Understanding is not only concerned with things which come under Faith primarily and principally, but with all things subordinate to Faith as well . . . certain actions, not as if these were its principal object, but inasmuch as the eternal law is the rule of our action. . . . The Holy Spirit, by the Gift of Understanding . . . enlightens the human mind, so that it knows some supernatural truth, to which the right will must tend. Some who have sanctifying grace may suffer dullness of mind concerning things that are not necessary for salvation, but concerning those that are necessary for salvation, they are sufficiently instructed by the Holy Spirit. . . . Faith implies merely assent to what is proposed, but Understanding implies a kind of perception of the truth, which perception, except in someone who has sanctifying grace, cannot concern the end. . . . The Gift of Understanding is concerned with the first principles of that knowledge which is conferred by grace; but otherwise than Faith, since it belongs to Faith to assent to them, whereas it pertains to the Gift of Understanding to penetrate with the mind the things that are said."

—*Second of the Second Part, question eight,* passim.

III
"More Beautiful than They"
The Gift of Knowledge

"More Beautiful than They"

The loveliness of lowly things is more than some hearts can bear. Enticed, enthralled, enraptured when their eyes see only a springtime world, they know only the light laughter of the living moment. No hint of hurt or harm—no hunger for another joy—shadows the brightness of their delight. When time is thus tender to their thoughts, marigolds and jonquils bloom together in their minds, and the morning of their pleasure knows no afternoon. The blandishments of beauty own them then—each little thing so lovable, their hearts are captive to the least.

When their hearts are yet in such blissful bondage, their minds are restless to be free. If they could but break the daisy-chain of sentimentality that binds them, they would be at liberty to know true beauty in the truth. Such knowledge of the truth in lowly things need not destroy, but may even sanctify their love. When men see things as they truly are, they love them as God Himself does—as His goods not their gods. Temples on the high places of their emotions may crumble and the idols of romanticism may be smashed, but their love of lowly things need be no less. They need not squint at beauty in pseudo-religious scorn. They look at it and love it in its full length, breadth, and depth—to the divine. If they know even the least of lovely, lowly things thus thoroughly, they cannot fail to "know how much the Lord of them is more beautiful than they" (Wisd. 13, 3).

Knowledge of the Lord of beauty is not a whispered rumor or an esoteric creed. It is the common monopoly of men. They alone of creatures on the earth have reason enough to revel in beauty. Eyes that are open and a mind that is aware, moreover, cannot miss the evidence of a Lord of beauty, "for by the greatness of the beauty, and of the creature, the creator of them may be seen, so as to be known thereby" (Wisd. 13, 5). Knowing the mass and maze of beautiful things upon the earth has been for many a distraction and a deterrent rather than a stimulant in knowing the Lord of beauty. The fascination of trifles has obscured the truth for them, and the more frequently they open their eyes to sensuous delights the more firmly they close their minds to their significance. Beauty becomes for them a new and heady wine, a savage and subtle power to destroy reason by absorbing it. Reason, however, if given a fair chance by a reasonable person, tends to abstract from the details of beauty and to assimilate its inner truth, and thereby to appreciate it the more. Such an appraisal is destructive neither to beauty nor to the mind. Flowers do not wither when their form is abstracted by the mind, nor is the reasoning mind warped with such adulation as "On your knees, man; here are violets." A just estimate of beauty and truth is not a rare stroke of genius, uncommon and unknown to the majority of men. Each mind has a share of it, and only a man who can see a kitten and deny the existence of a cat can know any effect without having an indication of a cause. That power to know, in fact, is so generally shared by men that, unlike wisdom, it has no special name but is called merely knowledge, or science.

The notion of science, or knowledge, has been artificially limited in academic circles. It has become more a process of action than a product of the mind. Any selected series of acts or phenomena observed in sequence may be the subject of scientific investigation, and the very search constitutes the science. Although this notion of knowledge or science is not universal, it is influential, and it has distorted many subordinate factors of education. Men think of science in terms of apparatus instead of the appreciation of truth; they imagine that a physicist's laboratory table or a psychiatrist's couch is more necessary to science than are keen perception and cautious reflection. Yet observation and reasoning are the vitals of science. They are both part of it and produce it, just as a heart and lungs contribute to animal life and are a part of it. In science the mind comes to a conclusion, and neither the coming nor the conclusion can be omitted from the integral notion of science or knowledge. Knowledge, moreover, is not a single act, but the resultant of several acts, a fixed habit. Such habits, sometimes called "circuits" by modern psychologists, are like paths in a jungle; they do not prevent excursions into experimentation, but they do provide a secure and well-marked way from principles to conclusions.

The journey knowledge makes is about halfway to wisdom. It leaves the habit of understanding poised on a knoll of principles, and points out the way; it crosses the broad fields of observation and experimentation, and it starts the climb to causes. It even reaches the top, the ultimate, but it cannot rest there. The privilege of being at home at the pinnacle of reality belongs to wisdom, which begins at the top of the mind and works its way down, and out through the tips of the fingers into practical effects. Knowledge adds analysis to the intuition of understanding. It not only notes a connection between cause and effect, it knows the reason for that connection. It even pursues that reason until it can go no further, because it has found the final answer, the ultimate cause. Its knowledge of the ultimate cause, however, unlike that of wisdom, is not intimate. In fact, it reverses the process of wisdom; knowledge judges the ultimate from all things, while wisdom judges all things from the ultimate. Wisdom sees creatures out of the corner of its eye; knowledge sees God behind their backs. The beauty behind the backs of things, the cause of things from the least to the last, is the peculiar concern of that ability to know with which mankind is much more commonly endowed than with common sense.

Because of many down-to-earth cares or much down-to-hell living, most men do not have the common sense to use properly the light of knowledge within their souls. They have the ability to know, but they are more likely to become machines for international business than to heed any admonition to think. Only a few, after a long time and with the admixture of many errors, have thought their way through the truths of nature to God. Such myopia, however, is not a result of television, theatres, or even troubled times. The pitiable record of human intellectual efforts, from the early pagan philosophers to the present authors of theories on the atom and the autonomy of the human intellect, indicates many sincere failures and much incredible folly. The text is clear in nature, but dull scholars must have it read to them through revelation. With unending patience God has repeated, in words of man's own making, truths men could know from their natural intellect and the nature of things, but which most would have to die to discover. By His revelation He has supplemented, but not supplanted, the action of the human mind. He has enabled men to see clearly the beauty of things and the Lord of beauty so that they may be more certain of what He says about the "things that are not seen."

The unseen things of the mysteries of supernatural revelation are basically the autobiographical details of God's Trinitarian life. The biographical data that can be had from the record in nature gives an understandable picture of the Simplicity, Perfection, Infinity, Eternity, and Unity of God; all, in fact, "the invisible things of him ... clearly seen, being understood by the things that are made" (Rom. 1, 20). His intimate life is, however, without revelation, as unknowable as His thoughts. Yet for those who have the facts of His life and the faith to assent to them, a wholly new album of unexpected and undeserved pictures and vignettes is open and available for quiet contemplation. This album of the author of grace is filled with accurate representations of Him through Sacred Scripture and Tradition; its borders are fixed in the teaching of His infallible Church. It offers men not just something to browse through on a Sunday morning with the children before the newspapers come, but a way of life, a reason to die, and a perfection of human nature through grace which can only be exceeded by the vision of glory.

Grace can supplement nature precisely because it is better stocked than nature. The Lord of beauty is no less bountiful in granting, sustaining, and perfecting supernatural life, than in doing the same for the natural. Whatever is found in nature is likewise found, not only in God Himself, but in His grace. Whatever God has given to His servants, He has not refused His sons. Just as the natural habit of understanding grasps first principles, and the natural habit of knowledge moves from conclusion to conclusion as from cause to cause, even to the ultimate, so the spirits of understanding and of knowledge are fixed factors in the soul's supernatural intellectual life. While understanding in nature penetrates the otherwise inscrutable face of nature, understanding as a Gift penetrates the unsearchable ways of God. Knowledge in nature, moreover, knowing nature's chain of causes, is utterly unaware of the supernatural sequence and dependence of events. That causal relationship the Gift of Knowledge lovingly analyzes to certify in souls the word of God, and confirm them in their Faith.

The confirmation of Knowledge is a coming of age through the Holy Spirit. The soul which has hitherto assented to the truths of Faith on the authority of God loses none of its basic trust when it lovingly inquires about the basis of that truth and every truth it holds. Its Faith is just as immense, stretching to the full area of supernatural revelation, but its interest is much more intense. Its inquiries are not prompted by mere meddlesomeness or curiosity, but by the moving Spirit of Truth. Coupled with inquiries about causes is a holy indifference about creatures in themselves. In an attitude of "Be it done to me according to thy word" (Luke 1, 38), the soul with Knowledge does not wish to cling to anything, even to the various graces it may previously have enjoyed. It desires merely to trace the causes of grace or any of the works of God, through the hierarchy of God's instruments, back to the Source of all life. Such inquiries require strength of mind and a restraint, a perceptive judgment, and a docility to truth; an analysis and at the same time an awe of mystery. Obviously, no one can discover for himself the correct measure and proportion of the elements of Knowledge by acts of Faith, Understanding, or theological trial and error. He has to be taught by the Paraclete.

The education of a loving soul through Knowledge involves not an exclusively passive assent, a nod when the whole class nods, but a personal judgment. Primary instruction in the facts of Faith is, of course, presupposed to the tutorial system of the Holy Spirit. The act of Knowledge, however, is the enlightenment of a single soul, enabling it to judge correctly, and for its own supernatural benefit, the various elements, effects, and explanations involved in a mystery. The act is a vital and willing one for the soul, even if it is not the result of long deliberation. In assent it has agreed to the knowledge of another, which remains in the other, but in the act of Knowledge, the truth and the soul's certainty, however great or small, are its own. Although not more valuable in itself than Faith, the act of Knowledge may seem more precious. For the most part it is better to own a lamp than to read by a lighthouse, especially if the latter will be lending its sweeping assistance anyway. By the personal possession of Knowledge, the soul is able to separate, as its sanctification demands, true opinions from false, the certain from the uncertain, what is to be believed from what is not, with regard to created causes in both the supernatural and natural orders. It has a judgment to fit its needs of the Humanity of Christ, the Motherhood of the Virgin, the causality of the sacraments, the advisability of vows, the value of education, and the loveliness of all lowly things, knowing that the Lord of them is "more beautiful than they."

In each of its judgments Knowledge provides certitude for only that soul which receives the moving force of the Holy Spirit. The Gift of Knowledge is not charismatic, not for the apostolate or for teaching others. A saint with Knowledge can perhaps never turn a phrase nor make a conscience twinge. In the face of error he can merely hold his own position. No forensic triumphs or even quiet conversions need crown his own personal certitude, yet with each experience of knowledge his own salvation is more secure.

The contribution of knowledge to salvation is not, however, that of a practical judgment, such as Counsel offers. Knowledge is more the mind's supernatural philosophical friend than its lawyer. It is first of all a speculative appraisal of general situations and areas of judgment; only secondarily is it applicable to issues and actions. Knowledge sees the causes of the countenance of things as they are; its business is not to change their aspect. Knowledge, for example, makes its own in an intimate and inimitable way the judgment that the resurrection of Christ, the new Adam, is the immediate cause of the resurrection of men, just as Adam's sin was the cause of the punishment of death, since "by a man came death, and by a man the resurrection of the dead" (1 Cor. 15, 21). The facts cannot be altered, but they can be analyzed, even to their practical consequences. This the Gift of Knowledge does, separating truth from falsity, and indicating the doctrinal basis of moral acts by the argument that "if Christ be not risen again, your faith is vain, for you are yet in your sins" (1 Cor. 15, 17). Adam's sin, Christ's resurrection, and the governing principles of every Christian life can be seen in Knowledge as intimately connected. For Knowledge, therefore, verification of the life of Christ precedes the sanctification of the lives of Christians; the facts must be true for their fruits to be good. Without giving again the argument from authority that belongs to Faith or the imageless evidence of vision, Knowledge does the next best thing: it gives the soul interior, incontestable, and truly scientific certitude of "the things that are not seen."

The certitude of Knowledge results from a judgment, but not from any human effort. No clinical or laboratory investigation of motives or results, no weighing of elements, balancing of factors, or formulating of syllogisms is possible. If time is lost in these things, the act is not that of Knowledge but of theology or some lesser science. Knowledge does not act in such a human, deliberative way, but in a divine mode—swift, calm, and sure. For certitude Knowledge must be analytic; it must see both the conclusions and their principles, both the effects and their causes. Otherwise, it would not be able to give the mind adequate support. Yet the supernatural Gift need not act in the same slow way as the natural habit. It need not draw the conclusions from the principles, nor work its way back to causes from effects. In imitation of God's own eternal, intuitive, intellectual operation, Knowledge, as something of the Holy Spirit Himself, apprehends principles and conclusions, causes and effects, not one from another but one in another. In this way it is instantaneous and intuitive. Its best physical parallel is the instinctive reflex reaction of a man, like a jet pilot, who decides without deliberating. The decisions of Knowledge do not fire machine guns or do anything immediately practical, but they do find reasons. In this they are scientific. Although there are no retraceable steps and no possibility of repeating the act for experimental purposes, to satisfy a Victorian mechanistic scientist or a scholastic theologian, the soul is certain of the conclusion it has, the principle from which it came, and the connection between the two. A woman, for example, may be quite sure that the suffering and death of Christ on Calvary have sanctified her married life through the Sacrament of Matrimony, yet she may be quite incapable of explaining this to others or of justifying to them her happiness and her hopes. Her certitude seems to some merely a matter of instinct or intuition; it may well be an inspiration of the Holy Spirit Himself, who enlightens her through love.

The love that enlightens the mind to judge of created things is not an affection for the things themselves, but Charity toward God. However sensually, or even supernaturally, lovable created things may be—one's own state of grace or the humanity of Christ—they attract the mind with Knowledge for another reason than the beauty of their own form. They are manifestations of God, and it is to Him that Charity is directed. When the love of a soul rises up to Him, His light shines forth on created things. Yet the soul does not abuse its love for God, does not become more friendly with Him, as a neighbor in supernatural life, to get a better look at His garden. Rather the love that has already bound the soul to God moves the mind to seek out new manifestations of God's love so that the soul will have reason after reason for returning to Him whom the heart desires. As a mother fondles baby shoes, Knowledge finds in finite things remembrances of Infinity, in lowly things reminders of their Lord. The world, in fact, becomes a sacramental. In the most fleeting of nature's goods, Knowledge is aware of an Eternal Cause—in a sunset, in a breeze. Things are the symbols of Divine Love. In a trickle of water, a sign of the Cross in oil, a few absolving words, Knowledge sees with inspired and intuitive clarity the grace-giving power of the Sacraments of Christ. The whole world becomes a wondrous thing, a place where the mind with Knowledge may roam but never rest.

Knowledge, however, is more of an analyst than an explorer. It forms its judgment of things on the basis of reports and records rather than through on-the-scene investigations. Judgments already formulated into theories or opinions, the briefs of Faith and natural knowledge, are the principal subject of its concern. It determines what is to be believed and what not, what is the correct appraisal of reality and what is not. Wisdom by its superior power ranges wide through the field of reality without ever neglecting its executive directorship, but Knowledge as a lesser functionary stays at home, balancing the accounts. This nuance is not negligible. The function of Knowledge is restricted so that it will not encroach upon Wisdom, but it is as necessary as any other Gift. Knowledge falls directly upon statements, judgments, and opinions, but it cascades down to the things themselves. These expressions of truths, near truths, or far-fetched falsehoods are themselves quite real. Errors and opinions have a way of jostling through the centuries and controverting the certitude of every mind. Sometimes, long after the event has passed, the judgment of minds about it endures. In judging judgments, therefore, Knowledge does not lose contact with reality but has a purer, more balanced, and more beneficial view of its inner truth. It has an inspired analytic judgment of the truth, a sudden stereoscopic view of all things from the very least to the most sublime. The act of knowledge, like "the sun giving light, hath looked upon all things," and concluded that "full of the glory of the Lord is his work" (Ecclus. 42, 16).

The pinnacle of God's glory in His work is not a sky-scraping construction of men but the "weakness" of One who came down from heaven. Of all possible objects of its consideration of created causes, Knowledge finds nothing more attractive, nothing more perfect, than the Humanity of Christ. His body is the archetype of creation and the consummation of the entire cosmos formed by the Spirit of Love Himself. His soul, like every man's except for sin, is the sanctuary of the supernatural, "full of grace and truth" (John 1, 14). From His plenitude, moreover, all the blessings of supernatural life are measured out to men, since "of His fullness we have all received, and grace for grace" (John 1, 16). Just as the Humanity of Christ as a whole and in its parts is subject to the analysis of Knowledge, so each of His acts and effects provides unending objects for its judgment. The soul of Christ is the instrument of every grace, and the source of all merit. His human intellect and will, by which He acted as a humanly free agent, were dedicated to the accomplishment of the Will of God. That Will is the redemption of men, and Christ "loved us, and washed us from our sins in his own blood" (Apoc. 1, 5). By His death, death itself was destroyed as the shroud of a sinful world. In His resurrection is the immediate cause of every reformation, "For although he was crucified through weakness, yet he lived by the power of God" (2 Cor. 13, 4), and He "will reform the body of our lowness, made like to the body of his glory, according to the operation whereby also he is able to subdue all things unto himself" (Phil. 3, 21). For an awareness of the effectiveness of the actions of Christ through His humanity, the interior intuition of Knowledge is better than a voice from a crucifix or from the tabernacle. The soul is certain through the Gift that the direct cause of every effect in its supernatural life is something of the life and death of Christ. Whatever has happened or will happen is His work. Each time the soul resists temptation, it is because of His triumph over temptation. Every supernatural act throughout life is attributable to Him, since "as Christ is risen from the dead . . . so we may also walk in newness of life" (Rom. 6, 4).

In the renewal of life, Christ is unique but not alone. The soul which, through Knowledge, can perceive that in Christ both His divinity and humanity do what is proper to them, one in communion with the other, cannot fail to grasp the subordination of other instruments beneath the Humanity of Christ. Because something essential to that Humanity originally belonged to the Virgin Mary, she, as the Mother of God, does what is proper to her in the scheme of salvation in communion with her Son. She is not only a monstrance of divine goodness, she is a mediator. Her virginal Motherhood of God and her spiritual motherhood of men are of the same moment in time and in the salvation of men. At Cana, her effectiveness in simply announcing "they have no wine" (John 2, 3) was a result of her having willingly heard an announcement made to her, and is, at the same time, the beginning of the public record of her intervention for mankind. On Calvary or in heaven, in suffering or in glory, the Son and the Mother are associated in the redemptive act and in the unending administration of divine grace. Those whom the Holy Spirit has thus joined in a physical and spiritual union beyond expression, the same Holy Spirit has not separated as objects of the Gift of Knowledge. Just as the guiding Spirit of the Church has kept it free from error about the Son by defending His Mother, and from error about the Mother by definitions concerning her Son, so in the interior infallible tribunal in which the Holy Spirit forms judgments for individual souls, the two are associated as sanctuaries and sources of grace.

Subordinate to His Humanity, yet inseparable from Him in the work of salvation, is His Church, "which is his body, and the fullness of him who is filled all in all" (Ephes. 1, 22). As a palpable and progressing organism, the Church, remaining one in all times, can increase in wisdom, age, and grace before God and men. From its infancy to its maturity it is under the constant influence of Christ, so that He may sanctify it by the laver of water in the word of life; that He may present it to Himself a glorious Church, "not having spot or wrinkle, or any such thing; but that it should be holy, and without blemish" (Ephes. 5, 26ff.). Made holy through Christ, the Church is itself a source of sanctity, purifying the mass of men.

Despite persecution of increasing fury, and defection of uncertain frequency, the spiritual energies of the Church are everywhere renewed and everywhere revivifying. The Church grows constantly "unto the increase of God" (Col. 2, 19). It preserves its trust by diffusing its treasure. Born from a dead man's side, it lives unto the end of time. Blessed by Christ, it blesses; sanctified, it sanctifies; formed by Christ, it forms Him in the faithful.

To the loving admiration of Knowledge, a look at the Church is another look at Christ, who "is the head of the body, the church . . . because in him it hath well pleased the Father, that all fullness should dwell; and through him to reconcile all things unto himself, making peace through the blood of his cross, both as to the things that are on earth, and the things that are in heaven" (Col. 1, 18-20). In the analytic judgment of Knowledge, the action of the head and of the members is one. The mystery Knowledge encounters involves not only a triumphant head but a militant body, acts of infinite merit by the head and applications of grace to finite souls. In one loving glance at the Church, Knowledge sees the Humanity of Christ and His Divine Person, since "this is a great sacrament; but I speak in Christ and the church" (Ephes. 5, 32).

Beneath the "great sacrament" of the union of Christ and His Church are the seven sacraments, through which Christ and His Church operate for the sanctification of souls. These sacraments are of interest to Knowledge because they are causes which have been caused, effects which are of themselves effective. Water washes, oil soothes, and bread nourishes, even in the natural order, but in the supernatural order these simple elements act as instruments for the transmission of grace to the soul. Because Knowledge is concerned with created causes even to the least, it concentrates its attention upon the sacraments as sources of grace, especially the great sacrament by which Christ is present in the Church. The soul with Knowledge can appreciate intimately the words of Christ Himself, "As the living Father hath sent me, and I live by the Father; so he that eateth me, the same also shall live by me" (John 6, 58). Therein Christ has expressed a relationship between the Deity and His Humanity, His Humanity and a soul, and the soul and its life. Briefly, Christ has summarized the supernatural objects of the Gift of Knowledge from the highest to the least. But ordinarily Knowledge proceeds in the opposite way; it begins at the bottom and ascends on high. It proceeds from effects to causes, from conclusions to principles, and it includes the natural as well as the supernatural order.

The objects and opinions on the natural order which may fall within the scope of the Gift of Knowledge are innumerable. All the created effects and causes which absorb scientists of all kinds attract the soul with Knowledge. What the natural habit of knowledge had discovered about creatures, the Gift does not cast aside. With incisive and inerrant judgment, Knowledge transfuses natural truths with a new light. The theories of Galileo, Newton, or Einstein would neither overwhelm Knowledge nor disturb it. They have their place in the Providence of God, as little signs of lesser contradictions. Knowledge would not pretend to pass judgment upon the mathematical or physical aspects of these theories, but it would immediately reject any or all of their implications that it found contrary to Faith. The whole of the natural order, moreover, contributes to the supernatural, as the many grains of wheat to make the host for the consecration and the many grapes to the wine. The complete perfection of the natural order, as a matter of fact, is not in itself, but in its being assumed and used by the supernatural. Otherwise it would end in itself, and in utter frustration. In the natural and supernatural order, moreover, all effects point to their causes, and the causes themselves indicate the Creator "Who . . . beautified the glorious works of his wisdom" (Ecclus. 42, 21) by allowing inferior causes to carry out His Will, either because of a necessity implanted by Him in their natures, or freely by a liberty preserved by Him when He moves them. In all of them Knowledge has innumerable starting points for its analytic intuitions, yet in no created thing does Knowledge rest. Above all, it knows that the "Lord of them is more beautiful than they."

The beauty of the world, moreover, is not boundless. Limitation is of the very nature of created loveliness. Just as not every part of the body can be an eye, not every thing in the universe can be the best. For the harmony of the whole there must be grades of goodness. God has made a world of replaceable and reciprocating parts, and He has made them all make the best of it. All created beauty together cannot last forever or ever be whole. Something is always lacking to each thing, so that another may contribute it. Yet the desired harmony of things is not always actually achieved, as one of the most obvious phenomena in the world, evil, can testify. Evil, however, is never alone; it is always associated with good.

From the good of things Knowledge can scarcely turn its gaze. Toward evil, Knowledge gives a quick but comprehensive glance. Like a house detective, Knowledge has the whole picture in a moment. It has met this kind of thing before and need not dwell upon details. Yet Knowledge under the Holy Spirit is very realistic about evil. Horrible murders, perfidious acts, "destruction upon destruction . . . and all the earth is laid waste" (Jer. 4, 20), lie open before it. It conceals nothing, condones nothing; nor does it confuse anything, but considers every aspect of things, from the undeviating movement of the earth to the devious motives of the earthly. Knowledge, no more than philosophy, can pretend to be a cure for a toothache or an earthquake. Yet it can couple with an awareness of the privations which constitute evils of all kinds the certitude that not one is without a purpose. The failure of the good things of God is part of the plan of the unfailing Wisdom of God. Shocked at evil each time it becomes aware of it, the soul with Knowledge is secure in God. It does not hide itself behind the skirts of platitude about the best of all possible worlds in which things are getting better and better—or at least becoming more of a bargain. Nor is the soul candidly cynical, content to cultivate its own garden, wishing a plague on privations and philosophers alike. It faces evil in the only way the human mind can, as a mystery, some of whose aspects it can know and others it cannot. Its solution may not satisfy a mother whose child has just died, or make good propaganda for a nation which has recently suffered defeat, but for them and for all, the analysis of Knowledge is the most perceptive and the most practical.

The judgment of Knowledge cleaves evil in two. Evil is a gelded good which may be either physical or moral. Physical good and evil are all about us. Through life and death, begetting and destroying, suffering and survival, good and evil are enmeshed. Yet the mind can disentangle physical evil long enough to know that it is a privation of a created good. Something ordinarily due to a creature is not there, although it clings desperately to some good in its weakness or wreckage. Moral evil, however, is a special case, and a greater, even if often less obvious, tragedy. By moral evil a rational creature deprives himself, not just of the perfection he might have from another creature, but of the attainment of God Himself. Sin, in the judgment of Knowledge, is more catastrophic than the blitz or bombs of men, or even the cataclysms of nature. It is suicidal to the soul. Deliberately by sin the soul casts aside not a particular good but All Good and its own life. In sin Knowledge finds the worst of evils and an effect so far from God that it is in no way attributable to Him. In evil, however, Knowledge sees an opportunity, although not a cause, for good, so that where sin abounded grace might superabound. The superabundance of grace is the restorative of the beauty of a distorted and disfigured world. Knowledge sees new beauty in deep lines of sadness that is salutary, in failure that is humbling. Most certainly the knowledge of evil in a supernatural light is a grace from God,

> instructing us, that, denying ungodliness and worldly desires, we should live soberly, and justly, and godly in this world, looking for the blessed hope and coming of the glory of the great God and our Savior Jesus Christ, Who gave himself for us, that he might redeem us from all iniquity,

and might cleanse to himself a people acceptable, a pursuer of good works (Titus 2, 11-15).

The good works of an acceptable people, who, as Knowledge makes the soul cogently aware, are cleansed of their sins by Christ, are principally the works of Christian piety. The Gift of Knowledge, therefore, gives the intellectual basis for the adoration of God "in spirit and in truth" (John 4, 23). The truth that underlies the Christian spirit of piety guards it from being either idolatrous or iconoclastic. Protected by Knowledge, the mind neither stacks shrines with symbols and images nor sweeps them away with a single backhanded judgment. It rejects all fetishes in medallions or monuments, and at the same time it would warm Protestantism's heart by filling its hands with reminders. Knowledge declares within each loving heart and head what the Holy Spirit has defined in the Church of the faithful: that images are vehicles of piety, not obstacles to it. For the long journey that devotion has to travel from a sense-dominated creature to a spiritual Creator, the transportation images offer is essential. In the Gift of Counsel the Holy Spirit controls the use of created things in the worship of God, but through Knowledge He grants them general approval for their psychological and supernatural value in leading the soul from the sight of things visible to a love of the invisible.

Knowledge makes of the symbols in Christian piety something perhaps psychologically less substantial and satisfying, but supernaturally more startling and stimulating. Homage cannot rest in holy water, or even in the Sacred Heart, but rises to the source of all sanctity in the holiness of God. A crucifix or picture is always translucent with the light of a Savior. All the solemnities in the approval of which the Holy Spirit has guided the Church may lose something of their pomp, but gain immeasurably in purpose. The solemnities of the Holy Sacrifice are courtesies to Christ and confessions of Faith. The chanting of the divine office is the whispering of spousal love. The preaching of the Word, the blessing of priests, the Rosary, and a myriad of other devotions bring something divine to the top of one's head or the tips of one's fingers and raise one's heart on high. In its own weakness and need, the soul with Knowledge has new reasons for wonder at the indulgence of God. With complete lucidity and candor, the soul knows that the very existence of further devotion may depend upon the externalizing of the present movements of the soul. As his body is necessary to life, so symbols and sacrifice are needs of growth in piety. With the absolute assurance of its own analytic judgment, the soul with Knowledge can affirm that lowly things can lift the heart to the loveliness of God.

Learning to love created goods for what they are worth, the soul must also learn to leave them. By holy violence, the Gift of Fear can drive the soul virtually outside itself and out of the world as well. In the warfare of the flesh and spirit, the Gift of Fear is the battle veteran and loyal protector. Knowledge is the strategist and economist. Knowledge conceives the plan and counts the spoils. It sets the general policy and many precise principles, and it gives to all mortification a motive. It points out the causal connection between living with Christ and dying to sin through penance: "For you are dead; and your life is hid with Christ in God. . . . Mortify therefore your members" (Col. 3, 3-5). Yet Knowledge makes of the mortification by which men bring their bodies into subjection not a ruthless killing but a kindly renewal. When the soul spontaneously submits to the superior norm of living a life with Christ that is hidden in God, any austerities are more than acceptable. Once the soul is convinced by the concrete personal experience of Knowledge about created things, it is far more consistent and controlled in its self-denial. Mortification is not just an obligation of corrupt human nature; it is an opportunity for chastising its childish sensuality so that the soul may grow to the full stature of Christ. On the other hand, Knowledge strips from the soul the comfortable mantle of Quietism, so that it cannot wrap itself up in its own righteousness and sleep its way through sensual dreams of perfection. Black puritanism and blank quietism have no part in the formation of the soul with Knowledge. Stiff upper lips and tightly shut eyes are not sources of sanctity; but a daily cross and a lifetime of abnegation are. For a soul with Knowledge, moreover, the problem of mortification is not acceptance but restraint, since as the soul begins to rise toward God it is more ruthless and relentless in clearing away obstacles. Then Knowledge must remind the soul that, while the world is meretricious, it has a meaning for those who can read the truth behind its lying lips. Knowledge makes the soul pause just long enough to be convinced it is time to leave.

Knowledge analyzes not only the passing scene, but the past as well. In the Cinderella saga of all things created, and especially in its own sinful story, the soul with Knowledge becomes aware of mingled joy and sorrow. If lovely things pass away, the soul is not disconsolate; by the grace of God, so do sins. When it loses what cannot last, it has found an unending joy in the Knowledge of limitless Love. A man with Knowledge is happy and in tears. He has the beatitude of Christ's promise and the promise of beatitude with Christ: "Blessed are they that mourn, for they shall be comforted" (Matt. 5, 5). Knowing the security of that promise and its fulfillment even in this life, the soul does not clutch each fading memory or claw at the present with indignant displeasure. Mourning the loss of what is human, it is comforted by the presence of the Lord of all.

The presence of God is comforting to the soul in the loss of good things in the world, but especially so in the remembrance of its own evil. The redemptive embrace of God for a soul that in the past has hurt itself and made itself homeless through sin is a comfort only experience can indicate. The stark fact of sin remains and seems even more horrible, but the assurance of redemption consoles the soul which mourns with penance. As an artist rejoices in rejecting the ugliness which revolts him, the man with Knowledge is comforted by his recollection of sins already purged from his soul through penance. He is not sullen or resentful that he has fallen and God has raised him up. Nor does he need or seek psychiatric treatment to explain his past by something previous. Rather, as his appreciation of his own responsibility for sin increases, his awareness of the work of the redemption and of God's mercy moves him to reflect upon the causes of grace and of all good things. He sees the very mourning for sin as the beginning of happiness, and the sorrow of his heart is irresistible to His loving Father, who blesses him eternally with vision, and even now with comforting Knowledge.

So long as that Knowledge remains in the mind, a petition for forgiveness cannot be absent from the heart. "Forgive us our debts" (Matt. 6, 12), "forgive us our sins" (Luke 11, 4) are not the dreary repetitions of morbid minds, but the daily prayer of those who have Knowledge. The soul with Knowledge has few illusions about itself; it knows its own weakness, its inclination to sin, its failure to satisfy for the past. It repeats its petition because of its almost hourly failures to fulfill the will of God, and perhaps because of its remembrance of some past hour when it has denied God completely. The regularity of the prayer is a cock's-crow reminder of its denials, and going forth from its self-satisfaction, the soul weeps bitterly. Yet if the soul with Knowledge mourns, it is not disconsolate. It has innumerable signs of God's mercy and power. The very fact that the soul is able, by the grace of God, "to forgive everyone" (Luke 11, 4) is evidence enough that whatever capacity men have of mercy is found superabundantly in God. It adds to its petition for divine absolution "as we forgive others" (Matt. 6, 12)—not as a limit for God's action but as a testimony of graces already given. If selfish men can be moved by grace to indulgence toward others, surely the Father of Mercy will place no limits upon His forgiveness.

Mourning that it has reason to ask for forgiveness, the soul is at the same time comforted because it has the grace to beg. Forgiven and comforted, the soul with Knowledge is always aware of its weakness, but is never overanxious.

Knowledge, which keeps a man from being fearful by disposing him to Fear, keeps him off the psychiatrist's couch and "on the go." He is not a worker, worrier, and wanderer, however; but he has a view of the future clear enough to prevent him from fumbling in the present. He is constant in his efforts without being too much concerned about results. He has the strength to see any task through, because he has the enlightenment to see through any truth. He has a world at his disposal, but never as a distraction. By being a man before God, he is like a god among men.

The "run of men," on the other hand, do not know where they are running. They do not look back, and dare not think what might be around the bend. They keep running away from terrors in the night or the more inescapable terrors within their souls. As a norm of perfection they have only prosperity; as an absolution for sin, suicide. They worry where the next meal or the next bomb is coming from, but they are little concerned with the coming of their Judge. They want to be at home in the world they love, with a fence around the future; and lacking this they are disconsolate, afraid to be ignorant of nature's power, and terrified at the consequences of relinquishing the grasp they have upon the things of the world.

With another love and another light, men with Knowledge walk with God. They have an abiding faith and an abundant love. They do not cling to truths which they do not dare to examine, but know the world well enough to defy its power to destroy their love. They are sure

> that neither death, nor life, nor angels, nor principalities, nor powers, nor things present, nor things to come, nor might nor height, nor depth, nor any other creature, shall

be able to separate us from the love of God, which is in Christ Jesus our Lord (Rom. 8, 38-9).

They love nothing God has made less than it should be loved, and they love the Maker more than all. On their lips there may be little laughter, but in their hearts there is abundant joy. In their work there may be nothing of the talent that is profitable in the trades of men, but on their minds there rests a spirit which teaches them the truths that are in the sight of God. They have, in brief, the science of the saints, which could make of the minstrel of God, St. Francis of Assisi, a true man of science. They have a lusty love of creatures which is the opposite of being lustful. They look upon the world with sober thoughts, but a loving heart. They truly love all lowly things which bear the mark of beauty from an all-lovable One ". . . more beautiful than they" (Wisd. 13, 3).

Knowledge
(*Summary from the* Summa)

"A twofold knowledge can be had concerning things to be believed. One, indeed, through which a man knows what he ought to believe, discerning matters to be believed from matters not to be believed; and in this manner knowledge is a gift and is common to all the saints. The other, on the other hand, is a knowledge about things to be believed, by which a man knows not only what he ought to believe, but he even knows how to manifest the faith, how to induce others to believe, and how to refute those who deny the faith. This knowledge is numbered among the gratuitous graces, which are not given to all but to some.

". . . the knowledge of divine things is called wisdom, whereas the knowledge of human things is called knowledge; that is the common name denoting certitude of judgment, and appropriate to the judgment which is formed from second causes.

". . . the Gift of Knowledge . . . primarily and principally, to be sure, concerns speculation, inasmuch as a man knows what he ought to hold by Faith; yet, secondarily, it extends to works, since we are directed in our acts by the knowledge of things of faith and of conclusions drawn from it. . . . They alone have the Gift of Knowledge who judge rightly concerning matters of faith and action, through the grace bestowed upon them, so that they might never wander from the straight path of justice."

—*Second of the Second Part, question nine,* passim.

IV
"The Seal of Resemblance"
The Gift of Wisdom

"The Seal of Resemblance"

Likemindedness is the climax of true love. Those who love each other find ever fewer the moments when their minds fail to meet. In the communion of their affection they discover a deeper communication and a more intimate conformity of thought. Thinking about the same things, they came to judge them in much the same way. Without destroying their distinctive personalities, they gain a new oneness of mind, which is neither exclusively intuitive nor completely analytic. In their loving union silence is more significant, and unspoken understanding more urgent, than articulate agreement. Joy in one another's presence, numbness in absence, are fundamental realities, since they live, not where they breathe, but where they love. Out of themselves by an exchange of hearts, those who love approach and attain the culmination of their friendship in intellectual identity.

Human love is at best but a shadow of the divine. Even lifelong friendships seem like the courteous nods of dinner partners compared to the intimate, eternal love of God for an immortal human soul. The consummation of the mutual friendship between God, who is Love, and the soul who loves is an ineffable intellectual identity, a beatific vision. In it the soul knows even as it has been known (cf. 1 Cor. 13, 12), and it is transformed to duplicate divine judgments. In that vision men see God "just as He is," and they are "like to him" (1 John 3, 3). Without losing their own personalities, they have no other dominant intellectual identity than the Divine Essence. They are, in fact, deified.

Deification through intellectual identity is never completely perfect so long as men "walk by faith and not by sight" (2 Cor. 5, 7);

yet it may be approximated. Through supernatural grace the soul, already formed in God's "image and likeness" (Gen. 1, 26) by its natural ability to know and to love, has a further resemblance to the Author of nature and of grace. By Faith it is able to assent to the things God and the blessed know in the evidence of divine light; by Charity it loves completely what it sees only in part, and, almost as if possessing it wholly, the soul "rejoices in the truth" (1 Cor. 13, 7). With both Faith and Charity the soul has a vital resemblance to the living God. Yet it may still act in a human and deliberative manner far inferior to the divine mode of acting possible to the blessed in heaven or those gifted by the Holy Spirit on earth. The soul is not deified even to the measure possible on this earth until it has the climax of its love, an intellectual likeness which duplicates divine judgments. That culmination comes upon the soul through the Gift of Wisdom, so that by the Holy Spirit the human soul is "full of wisdom and perfect in beauty" with a climactic "seal of resemblance" (Ezech. 28, 12).

The seal of divine life which Wisdom imprints upon the soul transforms it without destroying it, making of the soul "the unspotted mirror of God's majesty and the image of his goodness" (Wisd. 7, 26). With Wisdom the soul is imperturbably speculative and intensely practical. In an act of Wisdom the soul reconciles and reduces to unity the contradictions of a perfect Christian life in an all-too-imperfect world. By the seal of Wisdom the soul has a simplicity and a serenity, yet a scope and activity, that is inimitable by the most conscientious and concentrated human effort. The seal of wisdom eliminates nothing but sin, and it orders everything to God.

The ordering of Wisdom is the foundation of a Christian soul's simplicity and the seal of its resemblance to God. The simplicity of God to which the soul is likened by the seal of Wisdom is not a simplicity of imperfection but of perfection. It is not the mere capability of becoming anything, but the perfection of being everything. In a singular, incommunicable, independent way God is simple and one, and so is the soul with Wisdom. God is not one because there is not enough of Him to be multiplied, but because He is too perfect to be divided. "God is a spirit" (John 4, 24), and His simplicity and unity are not a matter of numerical count but a reality that transcends calculation and comprehension. Wisdom too is not only a simplicity amid the complications of human life, a hermitage for the mind, but a unified and ordered wholeness which is above and inclusive of all reality. Wisdom is not that simplicity of imperfection, the uncomplicated naïvete so lovable in children, which knows nothing of problems and possibilities. It is rather that superior unity and simplicity of spirit by which the soul is made "holy, one, manifold, subtile" (Wisd. 7, 27) by bearing the seal of God's simplicity upon the necessary complexity of human life.

The complications of human knowledge make the most intellectual of men seem lowbrow. Although they are cousins once removed of the angels in the way they know things, men have by nature only a distant relationship with God. They are not tethered by sense knowledge to particular sights and smells, but they cannot wholly escape the humble origin of what they know. They have to begin with sense data and often return to sense images, yet they can strip off some of the encumbrances of the shell of sense knowledge to get to the more simple inner elements of things. Once they have formed simple ideas, they have to compound them with other ideas to form sentences and arguments for their reasoning. The entire process of human thought, and consequently of human life, is an effort toward analysis for the sake of synthesis, and synthesis for the sake of simplicity. Yet the most perfectly simple human life seems hopelessly complicated and even confused to an angel.

Angelic knowledge makes its human parallel seem topsy-turvy. Men begin by looking at the outside of things to penetrate the interior, but angels turn things inside out or upside down to see the spiritual aspect first and the material as an afterthought. They seem to have a head full of answers before they meet the problems, yet they are not in the least unscientific, since true science is a matter of certitude not of struggle. They have all their ideas infused by God, and their method of knowing is intuitive rather than investigative. By nature they are more simple than men, precisely because they are more spiritual and because they share more perfectly the resemblance to the Divine Simplicity.

Simplicity is the dominant characteristic of the divine essence and of the divine intelligence. God does not derive His ideas from things or from any teacher; yet He knows under every possible aspect everything that was, is, will be, or could be. In fact, the ideas of God are identical with His intelligence, and His intelligence with His essence. According to a human manner of speaking, however, God sees Himself in an eternal, comprehensive vision of the Supreme Reality. Seeing His wisdom and His power, He knows the full extent of their effectiveness and all the effects that will eventuate in due time. He sees things other than Himself, moreover, not because they cause knowledge in Him, as they do in man, but because His thinking about them causes them to come into existence. This causative characteristic of divine knowledge is inimitable, but of the simplicity of His knowledge creatures can have some share. By merely thinking about it men cannot bring a thing into existence, but by thinking of all things as one under God they can unify their own ideas and imitate divine simplicity.

The natural likeness which men may develop toward divine simplicity is enhanced by supernatural Faith. In its enlightenment concerning the intimate life of God, in its awareness of the unity of the end of all creation, the soul with Faith is more like God as He is. The facts of Faith, the articles of the Creed, are not only additions to human knowledge but summations of it. Even if the various statements of Faith seem as fragmentary as the pieces of a stained-glass window, when the light of the First Truth shines through them they give a single impression of the color and meaning of all reality. The true meaning of all reality is in its end, and Faith tells the soul which is redeemed that "creation itself also will be delivered from its slavery to corruption into the freedom of the glory of the sons of God" (Rom. 8, 21). That glory is the single, supernatural consummation of all, when all things beneath man serve him and he serves God for all eternity. The mere knowledge of that supernatural end gives human thought and life a profound simplicity which the philosophers or political leaders could never present. Unless knowledge through Faith is perfected by Charity, however, the new resemblance to God which it gives the soul remains obscure and inoperative. It is like that of a sleeping, or even dead, child toward his father. The features are evident, but none of the activity. A dead Faith is not only a disappointing sight; it is actually ghastly, a likeness of the Living God that is not alive. When God is known by Faith as the end toward which all things tend, yet is not loved by the soul as its own end, the intellectual likeness the soul has toward God is a caricature rather than an image. An intellectual identity with God is all but lost, since he who does not love does not know God; for "God is love" (1 John 4, 9).

Knowing Love as He is, the soul has a living Faith. It has not a cold assent to a distant truth, but the affectionate acceptance of the abiding presence of God within itself. Through a Faith made vital by Charity, the soul knows that "God is love, and he who abides in love abides in God and God in him" (1 John 4, 16). The resemblance to God of a soul with living Faith is due to the presence of Simplicity Himself within it. God is not reduced to the narrow confines of the soul, but the soul is expanded to possess something of God Himself. In the fullness of Faith and Charity the soul becomes more like God than like its former self. Its judgments are still made in a human manner, but they are based upon divine principles; it deliberates and decides by reasoning from principles to conclusions rather than by enjoying an immediate intuition of conclusions within the principles themselves. Faith and Charity give the soul its most perfect supernatural resemblance to God, since they unite the soul to God and "he who cleaves to the Lord is one spirit with him" (1 Cor. 6, 17). Yet they leave to Wisdom the function of sealing that resemblance by its divine manner of acting through immediate intuition. Faith and Charity enable the soul to think of the same things God thinks of, and Wisdom enables it to think somewhat in the same way. All three enter into the climax of the soul's love with God in which it is "transformed into his very image from glory to glory, as through the Spirit of the Lord" (2 Cor. 3, 18).

The gradual "from glory to glory" transformation which the Spirit of the Lord effects within the soul is the intensification of Wisdom, which increases in an exact ratio to the perfection of Charity. "The charity of God is poured forth in our hearts by the Holy Spirit who is given to us" (Rom. 5, 5), and in the human mind the immediate consequence is a deeper disposition to be moved by the Holy Spirit to judge in a divine manner. Charity and Wisdom are more intimately joined than Charity and any other element in Christian life, since Wisdom is Charity's last and most beloved child. Charity is the mother of all the meritorious actions of Christian life, by begetting, nourishing, and fostering a varied progeny of good habits in their own proper acts. Charity gives these actions its own features and makes them pleasing to God, but it does not deprive them of a form totally their own. Acts of fortitude or chastity in the lower appetites, acts of justice in the will, or natural knowledge and Faith in the intellect are stimulated and controlled by Charity. Yet in each Charity remains, not aloof, but outside the habit itself. In an act of Wisdom, however, Charity does something mysteriously more. Love Himself acting through supernatural love within the soul enters into an intellectual judgment.

When love not only moves the mind to act but enters into the act itself, the results are ordinarily confused or even tragic. Love is not only blind, but blinding in prudential decisions which involve the beloved. Even speculative judgments may be so influenced by love, usually self-love, that a man cannot distinguish a prejudice from a principle. Yet when Charity and the Holy Spirit form a judgment, the mind is purified and the decision is clear and certain. In either the contemplation of divine things or the directing of things human "His anointing teaches us concerning all things" (1 John 2, 27). The unction of love is in itself an enlightenment.

The action of charity is not, moreover, merely a fixing of intellectual attention which would normally result in clearer knowledge. It is rather a bringing of the mind into the presence of its object. The intellect itself, by abstracting and ascending from creatures or by accepting God's revelation, may have God presented to it in an image, but this knowledge seems distant, an infinitely long approach to an inaccessible light. By Charity, on the other hand, the soul knows something just short of the face-to-face vision which will make it eternally happy. "I have found him whom my soul loves: I held him; and I will not let him go" (Cant. 3, 4), the soul exclaims under the inspiration of the Holy Spirit and because of its awareness of an almost contactual sensation of God. The difficulties of distance, obscurity, uncertainty seem to disappear, and for a moment at least the soul has a vivid awareness of the indwelling goodness of God.

The experience of an act of Wisdom is not, however, a reflexive analysis of the soul's spiritual state. It is neither a judgment of the state of grace, which belongs to prudence, nor an attachment to pious things, which pertains to religion. In Wisdom the soul is more aware of God than of itself, although "this also was a point of wisdom, to know whose gift it was" (Wisd. 8, 21). Although of another order, the inspiration of Wisdom is not totally unlike that of poetry. The inspired poet is neither the self-conscious artist nor the unconscious instrument of a higher force. Although expressions may seem to fall as ready-made hexameters into his mind, the poet formulates the judgment of artistic merit. He deals, moreover, in something akin to the stock-in-trade of the metaphysician, or even of the soul with supernatural Wisdom. The poet is not concerned with particular things, flowers in crannied walls or oceans rolling on, nor, on the other hand, is he dealing with universal and abstract ideas. Between these two—the individual and the universal—is a common notion made concrete, which is conceived as existing in the nature of things but confined to the nature of no one thing. Not between but above both universal and particular is the object of Wisdom, God Himself. As known in supernatural love, He is neither an abstract universal nor a limited particular, although He has the perfections of both and the limitations of neither. In Charity, the communion of its friendship, the love has an uncontestable yet indemonstrable awareness of His perfect existence and His enticing proximity. The soul knows "I AM WHO AM" (Exodus 3, 14) and perceives something of the totality of the existence of God.

The apprehension that the soul has of "HE WHO IS" (Exodus 3, 14), unlike that of poetry, is negative. The soul knows, through Faith, Love, and an act of Wisdom, more what God is not than what He is. Because the appropriate object of poetry is a created thing, or at least God as compared to a creature, it has a direct and positive perception of its object. Wisdom in its relationsl with "He Who Is" as He is transcends all created knowledge and expression. It can be neither epic in its narration of the marvels of God and His providence nor lyric in its praises. It can only heed His admonition to "be quiet and see that I am God" (Psalm 45, 11). In the quiet, calm passivity of the Gift of Wisdom the soul is poignantly aware of God's words to St. Catherine of Siena: "I am Who am, you are who are not." Its own comparative nothingness, the soul knows full well, and in loving contrast it is able to "taste and see that the Lord is sweet" (Psalm 34, 9). Wisdom, therefore, gives the soul a positive, personal, and penetrating judgment of a divine experience, but in describing that experience the soul is forced to exclaim: "Oh, the depth of the riches of the wisdom and of the knowledge of God! How incomprehensible are his judgments and how unsearchable his ways! . . . For of him, and by him, and in him, are all things" (Rom. 11, 33ff.).

Loving admiration for God and an ordering of all things to Him are two aspects of the one act of Wisdom. Just as "he who loves God should love his brother also" (1 John 4, 21), by the same commandment and the same infused virtue of Charity, so by the one simple act of Wisdom the soul has a loving experience of God and all things as ordered to Him. This comprehensive simplicity in a loving experience of all reality in One, which is the act of Wisdom, makes of it the "seal of resemblance" between the soul and God and distinguishes it from all the other supernatural virtues and Gifts.

Wisdom is distinguished from Faith because the latter remains, at least in tatters, upon the souls of sinners who have turned aside from God. Sinners are more or less aware of God over their shoulder until, with a shout of defiance or denial, they drive Faith from their souls. They assent to Faith and accept its truth without being completely assimilated to the divine likeness. Their souls wear a supernatural but somewhat grotesque mask, the dead image of the Living God. Even in those whose Faith is vivified by Charity, the act of assent of itself does not imply an intimate, rapturous embrace of the One to whose authority the soul willingly acquiesces.

Charity, moreover, which vivifies Faith and enters into the act of Wisdom, is not identified with Wisdom itself. It does not enlighten the mind by any such intrinsic illumination as the light of glory which enables the soul to see God face to face. It does, however, make the object of love present and bring it more in focus; in fact, it makes possible an immediate experience of the Beloved. Because of the intensity of love, moreover, other objects that might be distracting are eliminated. As an act of the will, Charity is radically different from Wisdom, which is in the intellect, however much it may be influenced by the taste of love to see that the Lord is sweet.

Like all the Gifts of the Holy Spirit, Wisdom is distinguished from Faith and Charity but inseparable from them. Just as the body and soul of a living human being are distinguishable but inseparable, so the theological virtues and the Gifts live together, or are at the same time lost. Wisdom, however, is distinguished from all the other Gifts because it has its own special and superior function in the relationship of the Holy Spirit with the soul. The distinction between Wisdom, Piety, Fortitude, and Fear is obvious. These latter Gifts are in the will or in the appetites, and they are exclusively for practical action; Wisdom is in the intellect, and more speculative than practical. As dominantly speculative or contemplative, Wisdom is distinguished from the practical Gift of Counsel, which directs human actions in a divine way. From the two remaining intellectual Gifts, Understanding and Knowledge, Wisdom is distinguished as the apex of a triangle from the two subordinate and supporting angles. Wisdom has within itself, and in a more unified way, all of the perfections of both Understanding and Knowledge, with the imperfections of neither. Both of the lesser Gifts fuse their actions into that of Wisdom, yet they are not destroyed but completed by it.

Wisdom, moreover, has its position as the principal part in the intellectual relationship between the soul and the Holy Spirit not by being divided against the other two Gifts or even by being added to them, but by including both of them in its act. The intellectual life of the soul in which Wisdom is dominant is not so divided into specific segments that each Gift would have both the complete essence of a loving experience and its full power. In this conception of the relationship of the soul and the Holy Spirit each of the Gifts would have a separate and perfect existence apart from the others; Understanding would be equal to Knowledge and Knowledge to Wisdom. The concept of the intellectual supernatural life of the soul would be divided into mutually exclusive sections just as the concept animal is divided into brute and man. Saints under the inspiration of the Holy Spirit would be specialists in one branch or another of the intellectual Gifts. In such an outlook upon the Gifts there is no one more important than another, since each has not only the presence of Love within it but His full power also. This view tends to divide the single spiritual life into departments and to minimize the simplicity of the soul's relationship with the Holy Spirit.

According to another conception of the soul's intellectual life under the Gifts, no one Gift acts without all the others, and the full power of the Holy Spirit is only in the aggregate of all. From this point of view, likewise, no one Gift would be more important than the others, and, in fact, no one would be important without the others. It is a somewhat mechanistic view of an organic relationship, and it tends to belittle the diversity of the ways in which the Holy Spirit operates.

The simplicity and the subtlety of the action of the Holy Spirit is best preserved by conceiving of the speculative operations of the soul as a single whole with three parts, of which one is the principal. Wisdom is that principal part in the supernatural intellectual life, just as Charity is in the meritorious acts of the will. In both Understanding and Knowledge there is the illumination of divine love, since the Holy Spirit acts through them, yet in neither of these Gifts is the fullness of the power of the Holy Spirit uniting the soul with God. In both Understanding and Knowledge, God is known as lovable, but known and loved from afar. He is not as immediately present, not as much the source of their judgment, as He is in Wisdom, which looks at God first and then at other things.

A parallel for this phenomenon of single spiritual entity with a principal part may be found in the soul itself. The concept soul may be divided into human or rational, animal, and plant; yet an existing human soul is one with subordinate animal and plant functions. The vegetative, or plant, function of absorbing food is subordinated to the sensitive function of absorbing sense images, and both of these are for the purpose of the soul's rational activity of absorbing ideas. By nature the hierarchy is established and the simplicity preserved, so that a man has only one soul but various contributing functions. In the highest of these is human life in its fullness, although each of the subordinate activities is part of human life. In much the same way as the rational soul dominates the lesser functions without either absolutely depending upon them or destroying them, Wisdom acts in relation to Understanding and Knowledge. They may operate independently of Wisdom, but they are not complete, nor are their findings reduced to simplicity without it. The penetration of mysteries, the judgment of created causes, are true spiritual perfections in themselves and give the soul a resemblance to God, but unless they are completed with a superior, simplifying, unifying Gift of Wisdom, the soul has not received its final "seal of resemblance" to God.

Just as the Gift of Wisdom is the dominant part within the larger whole of the soul's relationship with the Holy Spirit, it has within itself a principal part or act which makes it like God. God's knowledge is primarily speculative and contemplative, since the principal object of His attention is Himself—Supreme Truth, Supreme Goodness, and Supreme Reality. Secondarily, but not as a second thought, God is concerned with created things, which He causes by His practical judgment that they can and should exist. Sealed with His resemblance, the soul with Wisdom is primarily contemplative. It gazes in utter admiration at the majesty of God mirrored within itself. It is quiet and sees that God is present. It does not meddle with forms of prayer, meditations or imaginings, or even reflections of any kind, but is "assured, secure, having all power, seeing all things, and containing all spirits" (Wisd. 7, 23). If there is any movement of the mind, that motion is circular. It moves from one divine fact to another in order to encircle, if not to comprehend, "Him Who Is" and within whose existence is all perfection. In this contemplative act the mind does not descend to created things but enjoys the loving experience of the Divine Presence by revolving about a single concept, applying to it all other ideas of God. It sees in a simple, loving judgment the Triune God, simple, perfect, infinite, and eternal, as "Him Who Is."

The contemplation of "Him Who Is" as He is automatically overflows into a consideration of all that is because of Him. The mind with Wisdom is able "to know the disposition of the whole world, and the virtues of the elements, the beginning, and ending, and midst of the times" (Wisd. 7, 17f.). In this way, Wisdom is eminently practical, since its practicality is founded upon divine things judged in a divine way. "For wisdom is more active than all active things; and reacheth everywhere by reason of her purity" (Wisd. 7, 24). The mind with Wisdom may plunge in a straight line from a consideration of divine things to a practical human conclusion; it may go from a consideration of the mercy of God to the immediate need for mercy among men. It may inspire the most active of the saints to practical works in a manner far superior to human deliberation, since in the one simple act it "knoweth things past, and judgeth of things to come" (Wisd. 8, 8).

Wisdom may, on the other hand, move in a more leisurely, descending spiral motion, coiling down through all reality. In its path things fall into place, since its function is to order all reality. From the pinnacle of perfection which is God, the soul sealed with

His resemblance through Wisdom sees an expanding sweep of things all sharing in divine love and directed toward divine goodness. In its descent to the practical order, Wisdom loses none of its simplicity or serenity, since its total attention is addressed to divine things or the divinity in things. Stephen, the first to be put to the practical test of Faith in martyrdom, "being full of the Holy Spirit looked up to heaven and saw the glory of God" (Acts 7, 55). He then judged human actions and what he would suffer at the hands of his persecutors not as something done to him but as offenses against God and punishable by Him. He did not, moreover, have recourse to any cause of salvation less than God Himself, and he prayed, "Lord, do not lay this sin against them" (Acts 7, 59). In the spirit of true Wisdom, Stephen saw the "glory of God" offended by sin, yet manifested in merciful forgiveness because of a martyr's prayers. In the superior and simple view of Wisdom that looks to the "glory of God," an Understanding of the mysteries of sin and grace, a Knowledge of the created, meritorious, and prayerful cause of redemption, and a Counsel of what God wills at the moment were all present, since Wisdom "knoweth and understandeth all things, and shall lead soberly in . . . works" (Wisd. 9, 11).

In practical works, in speculative acts, together with Faith and Charity, and above Counsel, Understanding, and Knowledge, Wisdom is the culmination of true intelligent love, and toward God a "seal of resemblance." As an intellectual act it looks toward truth, and as a loving experience it is in contact with goodness, so that in Wisdom the soul experiences the true as good and the good as true, since it "tastes and sees" Absolute Truth and Absolute Goodness in God. In this way Wisdom rises above, and yet includes within its superior, simple view, all the acts which belong to both the intellect and the will. It is the closest approach on earth to the beatific vision and the happiness of heaven, "for her conversation hath no bitterness, nor her company any tediousness, but joy and gladness"

(Wisd. 8, 16). Wisdom, moreover, does not deal in abstractions and generalities nor, on the other hand, in particular details as such. Its concern is not something other than the object of Faith, which is the First Truth, or Charity, which is the Supreme Good, but it does treat of these in its own unified and unique way. In a simple, loving experience it knows truth, goodness, and all that is perfect as "Him Who Is."

The single dominant idea or experience of Wisdom is its relationship to the Supreme Good, whose nature is to exist. Love of any kind, from the divine to the most degraded, is ordered to goodness, and goodness is found only in existing things. Abstractions, like numbers, have not existence, and consequently no goodness in themselves. Thus two of its nature is not better than three because two aches are better than three. Yet, on the other hand, existing things are ordinarily less intelligible, because in the created order they are subject to change. Wisdom, therefore, looks to the unchanging Essence, whose whole nature is to exist. It recognizes in God's revealed identity, "I Am Who Am," the single dominant idea in all divine things and, in fact, in all reality.

Although Wisdom in this life has no more from Faith than the "evidence of things not seen" (Heb. 11, 1), it orders all reality under the concept of the Divine Essence, "He Who Is." In order to contemplate that Essence, the soul with Wisdom must circle about it to see in a refracted light the single fact too pure for it to grasp without the beatific vision. It sees "Him Who Is" in the various ways in which He has revealed Himself as existing. It sees Him existing as One and Three, as Father, Incarnate Word, Invisible Sanctifier, and as Final End of all creation.

Wisdom's loving experience of God as One centers on the Divine Essence, "He Who Is." Since nothing can be added to the concept of Perfect Being, Wisdom sees at once that God is not a compound of various things, like a body and soul, or matter and form, or even the subtly distinguished essence and existence of all things that come to be and can pass away. In Him there are no unrealized capabilities, no inactive tendencies, nothing lacking, nothing left to be acquired. His simplicity is perfect, and His perfection, although inclusive in an eminent degree of all perfections of goodness, truth, and beauty, is altogether simple. The nuances of God's being, at once simply perfect and perfectly simple, are included within Wisdom's single intellectual experience of God's Infinite Goodness. God's Infinity is an existence which does not start where the stratosphere ends, but includes all things in the immensity of His Being. It is likewise changeless and beyond the measure of time. His eternal, infinite, perfect, and simple existence is unrivaled by anyone, and "He Who Is" is One.

"He Who Is," moreover, is not an inert being but an intelligent and free agent, a Person. He is "one God and Father of all, who is above all, and throughout all, and in us all" (Ephes. 4, 6). He exists as God and Father by His knowledge and love, His mercy and justice, and especially by His providence. "He Who Is" is "above all" by His divine manner of life; "throughout all" by His provident care of all things from beginning to end; and "in us all" by the special supernatural life that He gives to those who know and love Him by His grace. Without a shred of pantheism which would make of God a part or an aggregate of the things of nature, Wisdom sees things as sharing in His existence and His goodness because He has freely willed to create them. Because He is good, all things are, and in the measure in which He shares His goodness and existence with them they are better, as more like Him. The climax of that sharing in God's existence and goodness is in Charity and Wisdom, by which the soul bears from God a "seal of resemblance."

In its single simple judgment of "Him Who Is," moreover, Wisdom, based upon supernatural Faith, sees a far more intimate activity of God than His creation, conservation, governing, and perfecting of creatures. Wisdom is aware that the One God is Three in Person, Father, Son, and Holy Spirit. If the soul with Wisdom finds itself unable to express its experience of the ineffable reality of the Triune God, it also finds it impossible to conceive of Him otherwise. The Goodness of God, of which Wisdom has a loving experience, of its very nature tends to pour itself out to others, yet God can of necessity love only those equal to Himself. In the communication of Divine Goodness among the Persons of the Trinity, Wisdom perceives blindly, weakly, but no less lovingly, the intimate, eternal, necessary, activity of "I Am Who Am." From what it knows from Faith that the Son said of Himself, "I proceed from the Father" (John 8, 42), and likewise "the Spirit of truth who proceeds from the Father" (John 20, 26), Wisdom is aware of an origin of one Person from another without dependence of one upon the other. It knows and loves as One, Three coequal, consubstantial Persons, and it seeks to express to itself the distinction and relationship of Persons in a Oneness of Essence. Nowhere in nature can it find a more apt analogy than in the acts which remain within an intellectual agent. These are two, to know and to love. As God the Father eternally knows Himself, He begets His Son, to whom He eternally says: "This day have I begotten thee" (Psalm 2, 7). The Son, who is "the image of the invisible God" (Col. 1, 15), is generated not by an action in any way resembling carnal generation but at least distantly like the begetting of an intellectual idea, the formation of a word. In that intimate activity which is the procession of the Son by generation, Wisdom sees that the "Word was with God, and the Word was God" (John 1, 1). God, as are the Father and Son, the Holy Spirit is not generated but proceeds as a spirit, a breathing forth of mutual Love between the Father and the Son. He is the bond of Love, the primal Gift by which the Father and Son communicate the Divine Substance, and upon whom every other gift in heaven and on earth depends. He is One with them in nature as

"He Who Is," but He is identified with neither in His distinct relationship to both as the common source of His procession.

Within its simple view of the divine procession as the intimate life of the Trinity, Wisdom sees further "the grace of our Lord Jesus Christ and the love of God (the Father) and the communion of the Holy Spirit. . . ." (2 Cor. 13, 13). By a kind of fittingness only Infinite Wisdom could comprehend, the sending of Divine Persons into the world for the redemption and sanctification of men is related to the eternal processions of one Person from another. Although the Father comes to dwell in the soul in grace, He is nowhere in Sacred Scripture referred to as being sent. He rather "so loved the world that he sent his only begotten son" (John 3, 16) to satisfy Divine Justice and to express Divine Mercy. In like manner both the Father and the Son sent the Holy Spirit as an emissary of divine sanctification and a consort of the soul's supernatural life, "another Advocate to dwell with you forever, the Spirit of Truth, whom the world cannot receive. . . ." (John 14, 17). In the visible sending of the Incarnate Word, in the invisible sending of the Holy Spirit, or in the indwelling of the Three Divine Persons, Wisdom does not see a new existence added to Divine Life, but sees rather that the naturally ever-present God is in the soul in a new way, which changes the soul rather than God. That change takes place with each increase of grace in which the soul is more and more like God, more assimilated to the Triune Supreme Good, in its knowledge and love, of which the Gift of Wisdom itself is the seal.

Without straining to fit concepts into place, but by unfolding the single, simple concept of God's infinite existence as "He Who Is," Wisdom knows all that is knowable on earth of divine things. It is at the same time poignantly aware that "eye hath not seen, nor ear heard: neither hath it entered into the heart of man, what things God hath prepared for them that love him" (1 Cor. 2, 9). Yet of what it can know from intimate, loving experience, it is certain;

and from its certitude of divine things it draws forth practical and inerrant judgment of all things human.

The decisions of Wisdom may at times seem idiotic or evasive to those whose minds are too timorous or sensual to accept a radical solution to practical problems. Its solutions, moreover, are beyond the grasp of even the supernatural Gift of Knowledge, which is concerned with causes close at hand. Wisdom, leaving to other acts of the mind the work of filling in details, seeks and sees the Ultimate Highest Cause in all things. The Apostles had a particularly difficult theological problem when they asked Christ, "Rabbi, who hath sinned, this man, or his parents, that he should be born blind?" (John 9, 2). As they phrased the question they expected Christ to choose between two proximate causes. He, however, denied their alternatives and found the solution in the Supreme Cause alone, in divine glory: "Neither has this man sinned, nor his parents, but the works of God were to be made manifest in him" (John 9, 3). There is something more beneficial in Christ's words of wisdom than in His manifestation of power by working a miracle to cure the man born blind; yet both wisdom and power are one in God and in the loving experience of the Gift of Wisdom. In the miracle Christ gave the man the sight of a natural world of beauty; by His words He gave many men an insight into the supernatural beauty and practicality of wisdom. His works gave joy, His words gave peace, and both belong in a special way to Wisdom.

The peace which is appropriate to Wisdom is a pervasive attitude of mind, more than it is a result of the solution of particular problems. Wisdom is well aware that in this life there can be no totally perfect peace in which no desire would be left unfulfilled. Yet there can be true peace when the soul adheres to God and is "one spirit with him" (1 Cor. 6, 17). The happiness Wisdom attains through peace is not, however, something to be hoarded, but a blessing to be shared. Like the Charity upon which it is based, the peace of Wisdom must be shared or it will be lost. When the soul has a tranquillity of divine order within itself, it is zealous to establish that order in the whole world. It seeks to merit its final inheritance by pouring forth its present happiness. What it has received without guile, it communicates without envy and has as its guide the words of Incarnate Wisdom: "Blessed are the peacemakers, for they shall be called the sons of God" (Matt. 5, 9). Being called the sons of God, being "foreknown by God and made comformable to the image of his Son" (Rom. 8, 29), the soul with Wisdom can withstand in complete tranquillity of spirit its daily cross and final crucifixion. Its peacemaking is not a matter of political compromise but of sound social judgment based upon its vision of a provident God. "The multitude of the wise is the welfare of the whole world" (Wis. 6, 26) because they see the world as a whole and as a continuance of God's creative act. They do not minimize the significance of the least of events, nor do they oversimplify the greatest. They retain something of the "fear of the Lord that is wisdom" (Job 28, 27), and they recognize that much discussion of opinions and many prudential steps must be taken to reach even that tranquillity among men which is possible in this life. Yet Wisdom establishes something more than well-wishing, something more than concord. It quiets dissension, eliminates hatred, overcomes indifference, and deprives envy of its force, by ordering all things to their source and final end, to the one Being whose total nature is to be and to be good, "He Who Is." The Wisdom of the Holy Spirit is at constant warfare with deceitful self-love, which orders all, God included, to the individual, and which "is not wisdom descending from above: but earthly, sensual, devilish. For where envying and contention is, there is inconstancy, and every evil work" (James 3, 15-16). The Wisdom of the Holy Spirit, however, "will not enter into a malicious soul, nor dwell in a body subject to sins" (Wisd. 1, 4). On the contrary, "the wisdom that is from above is first of all chaste, then peaceable, moderate, docile, in harmony with good things, full of mercy and good things without judging, without dissimulation" (James 3, 17). Endowed with these characteristics by Wisdom, the soul acts in a way worthy of an adopted son of God and comformable to the image of God's divine Son. It enjoys the beatitude of being called, and truly being, a son of God.

The happiness of being of the supernatural family of God permeates the soul's every action and produces within it distinctive fruits of peace, charity, and joy (cf. Gal. 5, 22). Living according to these fruits, with a constantly renewed sweetness and delight, a man is able to regulate his own life and his relationship with others. Within himself he has a moderation of judgment in practical matters, so that he neither grasps at worldly expedients nor hesitates to accept extremes demanded by the inspiration of the Holy Spirit. He is docile to the Holy Spirit, and consequently to others through whom the Spirit may speak. In his Wisdom, moreover, he makes life more livable for others by being "in harmony with good things" and not aloof or opinionated. He contributes what he can, because he is "full of mercy and good things," which he pours out to others under the direction of the Gift of Counsel. "Without judging, without dissimulation," he presumes that others are good and presents himself as he is, and he is neither suspicious nor hypocritical. Aware that Wisdom has always "delivered from sorrow them that attend upon her" (Wisd. 10, 9), he can never lose the joy that bursts forth from a soul blessed with charity and peace.

In the joy of his peace and love, a man with Wisdom utters a canticle of petition and of praise. Although he asks for nothing for himself and can offer nothing to God, he expresses his desire that God may be praised as He deserves, and in a manner that only the angels and saints can approximate. He raises his mind and heart to heaven and by Wisdom, "seeing the heavens open and the glory of

God," he prays in union with the community on earth and the court in heaven: "Our Father, who art in heaven, hallowed be thy name" (Matt. 6, 9). In hallowing the name of God, the man with Wisdom is mindful not of his own designations for God as One, Immense, Eternal, Unchangeable, Infinite, Perfect, and Simple Being, but of all these together in the name that God gave to Himself in speaking to Moses, "I Am Who Am" (Exodus 3, 14).

In the quiet of contemplative prayer, a man with Wisdom repeats and relishes the Holy Name, "He Who Is," and recognizes in his act a simplicity, universality, and practicality that give to his soul its final seal of resemblance to God. He knows that he has reached the climax of true and divine love in the likemindedness of Wisdom from the Holy Spirit, which "being but one . . . can do all things; and remaining in herself the same, she reneweth all things, and through nations conveyeth herself into holy souls; she maketh the friends of God . . ." (Wisd. 7, 27).

Wisdom
(*Summary from the* Summa)

"He who knows the absolutely highest cause, which is God, is called wise absolutely, inasmuch as he can judge and order all things through divine rules. Man attains judgment of this kind through the Holy Spirit. . . . The wisdom which is called a Gift of the Holy Spirit differs from that which is an acquired intellectual virtue, since the latter is obtained by human effort, while the former is descending from above (James 3, 15). Likewise it differs from Faith, since Faith assents to divine truth in itself, while it belongs to the Gift of Wisdom to judge in accord with divine truth.

"Accordingly it pertains to the wisdom which is an intellectual virtue to pronounce correct judgment about divine things after reason has made its inquiry, but it pertains to wisdom as a Gift of the Holy Spirit to judge rightly concerning them because of a connaturality with them. . . . Consequently, wisdom which is a Gift has its cause in the will . . . Charity, but it has its essence in the intellect, whose act is to judge rightly. . . . From the very fact that wisdom as a Gift is more excellent than wisdom as an intellectual virtue, because it attains to God more intimately, by a kind of union of soul with Him, it is able to direct us not only in contemplation but in action as well. . . . The result of Wisdom is to make the bitter sweet and labor a rest."

—Second of the Second Part, question forty-five, passim.

V
"Let It Be So Now"
The Gift of Counsel

"Let It Be So Now"

Once upon a time there was a certain man without a doubt. Then a serpent spoke.

Fabulous as a man who was totally sure of himself may seem, he was a fact. With the companionship of God and His counsel, he ruled himself and his empire. His intelligence was unrivalled by anyone who might later measure his skull, and his judgments were inerrant. He was unashamedly naked of any artificiality, and he communicated his joyous confidence with her who shared his rib and his reason.

His "helper like himself" (Gen. 2, 20), however, brought him both his first human joy and his first problem. Eve offered Adam not only an apple but an opinion. For the first time, Adam heard advice other than God's, and he hesitated. His curiosity was aroused by the devil's promise that his eyes would be opened (Gen. 3, 5), since he thought God had given him as much knowledge as one human head could hold. The prospect was tantalizing. Such omniscience, Adam knew, was something just short of omnipotence. The desire to snatch the independence and excellence of divine prerogatives, to be on his own in decisions, swelled within his mind and upset the balance and subordination grace had established. Adam wavered, and then he plunged headlong into pride. Adam was, moreover, truly concerned about not offending his wife, who was all the world to him. He worried how he might observe the prohibition of God and please Eve. He tried to accommodate the law of God to his life rather than conform his life to the law. For Adam and mankind it was a crucial test, whose solution is in the Cross, and Adam and his progeny attempted to be "as gods" by insubordination rather than by grace.

The words Satan had conceived in the woman's mind brought doubt into the man's, and from Adam's weakness death entered the world.

From then onward, at least until time's fullness, men hid themselves in hesitance or ran naked away from truth. From one another they had learned evil, and at every turn of thought or action the lesson was repeated. Seldom again would men see anything as an unmixed good, and almost every decision concerning their own happiness left their souls limp with doubt. They had, it seemed, henceforth only the choice of enduring evil or inflicting it. Each man was troubled within himself and about himself to the point of murderous hatred, and like Cain he became "a vagabond and a fugitive on the earth" (Gen. 4, 14). Settled together in tribes or in towns for survival, men retained the nomadism of their motives, since "the thought of their heart was bent upon evil at all times" (Gen. 6, 5). With a relentless, ruthless, and revengeful spirit they tried to determine for themselves what would make them happy and how they should attain it. A flood of punishment, repeated and perpetual covenants, the chastisements of exile, promises and prophecies, and even the pedagogy of the Law did little to restrain them or restore to them the essence of paradisiacal peace, with its certitude of judgment and consistency of life.

Where the covenant and the Law failed, Wisdom Incarnate and Love Indwelling succeeded. Two Divine Persons, sent to dwell among men and within their souls, complete superabundantly the promised restoration for which the career of God's chosen people was a humbling preparation. Judged statistically, even the Incarnation of the Son and the invisible coming of the Holy Spirit might seem incomplete. Judged by its spiritual sufficiency, however, the redemptive and restorative action of the Divine Persons was more than adequate. It re-established the peace of divine confidence in man, even if it did not reinstate him in the paradise of delights. The actual application and reception of the light and love of Christ has never been universal, "but as many as received him, he gave them the power to be made the sons of God" (John 1, 12). Being the sons of God was not a mere title to an inevitable and eventual inheritance, but a way of life. "For whosoever are led by the Spirit of God, they are the sons of God" (Rom. 8, 14).

Those led by the Spirit of God lose nothing of their liberty, but all of their doubts. In them an aggressiveness born of hesitance may no longer be in evidence; instead, an intense consistency fostered by divine assurance takes its place. They are not less prudent in their actions, but far less impetuous or indifferent. In their passivity to the Spirit they are less deliberative about means, but they are far more dedicated in using the means He indicates to attain their ends. They have by divine gift what Adam once tried to steal, a share in God's omniscience—the Gift of Counsel. With a quickness and sureness it could never otherwise have, even after the greatest practice in prudence, the soul with Counsel leaps up to do the will of God, instead of plunging down into pride by doing its own. In a single simple intuition, under the enlightenment of the Holy Spirit, the soul sees, as far as is opportune, the end of its action and the means which are best adapted to the circumstances. In giving counsel and receiving it, in extraordinary and ordinary actions, the soul with Counsel has both a docility before God and a determinateness before men which only the inspiration of Indwelling Love can explain.

An unhorsed Saul was inspired to seek counsel, so that he might later give commands as God's Apostle to the Gentiles. Also John, sanctified by the Spirit even before his birth, had the counsel of the Spirit to ask and fulfill the work of Christ at His baptism. When the Lamb of God appeared before him at the Jordan, John had baptized many. Yet in Christ there was something utterly unique. Was the redeemer who took away the sins of the world to be subjected to an action which of itself did not take away sin but only reminded sinners of repentance? The Lord of the Sabbath, who had been circumcised to fulfill the Law, needed no sanctification, no exhortation to renewed faith in God's covenant. Even the supernatural prudence of John, who was no reed shaken by the wind, could not grasp the congruity of such an action. In the Spirit of Counsel John asked, ". . . comest thou to me?" Christ's reply and John's compliance are both indicative of the inspiration of the Spirit, removing doubt, determining an action but never revealing more than is necessary for the fulfillment of God's will. Christ said, and John did: "Let it be so now" (Matt. 3, 15).

For the moment or for a lifetime, such a divine assurance of Counsel is enough. So long as the soul has an interior appreciation of the will of God in its action, however mysterious and bizarre its workings may seem to natural prudence, it is "in darkness and secure." Although it remains in darkness, because in this life the soul still walks in Faith, Counsel leaves no doubts. Peter, "filled with the Holy Spirit" (Acts 4, 8), by the simplicity of his arguments and the constancy of his will confounded the Jewish council, whose motives and prudential norms were completely mundane. Yet at another time the same Peter, with supernatural prudence, was "doubting within himself" (Acts 10, 17) concerning a vision. Suddenly the "Spirit said to him . . . Arise . . . doubting nothing" (Acts 19f.). As soon as the Holy Spirit moved him to act, and not before, Peter had a certain interior judgment which gave him confidence that he was fulfilling the will of God. Counsel did not provide Peter with a full report of what the results of his "doubting nothing" would be, but it gave him the intellectual conviction that, despite his previous judgments, he should "let it be so now" and accept Gentile neophytes. No other course seemed reasonable, no matter what the consequences among his friends and followers might be. Like Peter, the other Apostles, and many Christians since, "were all filled with the Holy Spirit, and they spoke the word of God with confidence" (Acts 4, 31). When the test came, as it must to every soul which is aware of the contradiction between the will of God and the ways of the world, Peter, the Apostles, and every soul with Counsel is prepared to live and die in the principle that "We ought to obey God rather than men" (Acts 5, 29).

Obedience to God is at once the greatest of human sacrifices and its most trenchant perfection. Complete obedience is the work of Counsel. In its scope are works more pleasing to God than acts of sacrifice performed in the virtue of religion, and from it proceed acts which rise above not only the perversity of men but even their best efforts. At its very best the human mind has a fixed objective—an intense desire for happiness—and an enlightened free choice of means to attain its end. The desire itself cannot be destroyed, but the means to attain it can be completely distorted. Happiness can be identified with nothing further afield than the green grass next door, and the practical intellect, with serpentine scheming or bullish impetuousness, tries to overcome or undermine any moral barriers to its possession. Once the grass or any other created good is gained, the soul is not satisfied, and looks again for something else. Over and over again the mind changes its final end, and tries to adjust to it a new set of means. With each new experience it is less sure of itself, a little more indifferent and appreciably more inconsistent, since "a double minded man is inconstant in all his ways" (James 1, 8).

This duplicity of mind arises principally from pleasure-seeking. Sensual satisfactions delight, distract, and then destroy a person's judgment in practical matters long before they obliterate his science or judgment of speculative or practical principles. In each sin his mind retains the rules of conduct, but it does not apply them. In a kind of stupor the mind finds itself unwilling, or by habit incapable, of applying its memory of the past to the judgment of the present in view of the future. It casts aside its accepted principles rather than apply them to the current situation, because it is not sufficiently concerned about the consequences of its action: "Eat, drink and be merry," for science has a remedy for hang-overs and hell. Only the moment, or the past in dreams and the future in desires to be currently enjoyed, concerns the person imbruted by sensuality, and his only counsel is the impulse to grasp and gulp down every pleasure within reach. Yet in each sensual act a man's mind is a little queasy, since what his practical judgment demands at the moment, his other mind—his judgment of principles—has rejected for all time.

Another less common but no less uncontrolled source of a double mind and a doubting heart is avarice. With two heads and no heart, the avaricious are excessive in their prudence, rather than inept. They ignore the wise man's admonition: "Labor not to be rich; but set bounds to thy prudence" (Prov. 23, 4), and they put a fine edge on their reasoning powers at the grinding wheel of many sacrifices. Sacrifices are made, moreover, not only to gain wealth but to get one's own way. More subtle than the avarice of wealth is the avarice for dominance. There may be no recognized stock market for idiosyncrasies and neuroses, but the curb exchange and conniving for control is constant. Assuming authority, absorbing attention, minding other people's business—these things often give a perverted soul a tidy sum in self-satisfaction. Many sacrifices of honor may have to be made, and the soul may have to engage in adroit maneuvering, now being obsequious, then offended, but the eventual possession of the emotional strings which make puppets of other people seems worth it. In either avarice there is a caricature of prudence and a contradiction to Counsel. The motives for avarice are as much a part of carnal prudence as sensual delight. Its methods—astuteness, fraud, and deceit—are far more ruthless. Astuteness formulates the stratagems, while deceit and fraud carry them out. Once in a while deceit and fraud may bring upon an avaricious person discovery red-handed, and red-faced embarrassment, but his astuteness will remain untouched until humility, justice, courage, and temperance deprive it of a motive, and natural or supernatural prudence replaces it as commandant of practical action. Although not as complete as the control of Counsel, prudence in a human way teaches how the soul may obey God rather than men. It codifies the past and clarifies the present, and it offers the soul the best humanly available norms for action.

Prudence is, moreover, the virtue of the vigilant. Half-awake or half-aware, the soul cannot know a good means when it sees one. The soul's disordered inclinations to sensuality, timidity, or injustice may be put at rest by temperance, fortitude, and justice. Yet unless prudence is watchful about the means for keeping them in bondage, a struggle with temptation may arise which is stronger than could be imagined. In a positive way, also, prudence tries to find opportunities for the exercise of moral virtues. In it the speculative principles and general motivation of justice, fortitude, and temperance are made concrete. These virtues are concerned with the purpose of moral acts; prudence, with their performance. Prudence guides and guards the moral virtues by discerning the good and evil of various circumstances in which acts are to be performed.

In the judgment of these circumstances prudence has a knowledge more complex, and consequently not as certain, as sciences which deal in unchangeable truths. In every act there must be a remembrance of the germane facts of the past and a judgment of present circumstances. Raising an eyebrow or raising a family differ in many ways, but both may be subject to all the factors involved in prudence. Because it is impossible for anyone to know all he should to make his judgment prudent, a foresighted man is docile to the hindsight of others. Their trials are his erudition. He makes his choice of means, moreover, not in a cloister of abstraction, but in current and changing circumstances. If his decision is not to be frustrated in the doing, he needs circumspection and caution as integral to his prudence. By these he can bring his act to completion as he intended it, and he can avoid the impediments that the wiles and wills of others may present. In any single act he moves rapidly from taking counsel with the past to being cautious about the future, but he can omit none of the parts of prudence if he is to preserve prudence itself or the moral virtues.

All the methods of natural prudence are found in the supernatural virtue of the same name, but there is a new motive. Because the end of Christians is higher than that of those who do not live as the sons of God, their choice of means will also be different. Christian justice does more than give to another his due; it returns good for evil. In each case the Christian must decide exactly what good is appropriate to each evil—a loving blessing, a fraternal correction, silence. Likewise Christian fortitude does not stop at the border of the call of duty but crusades against every enemy, especially self-love, not only to an uneasy truce but to utter destruction. For Christian temperance, moreover, the prudent middle ground is not merely such abstinence and sobriety as health demands but a chastisement and a subjection of the body to the full service of the soul. Such supernatural virtues require a fountainhead in a supernatural love of God, above all else, and a supernatural prudence which alone can select the appropriate means to fulfill such exalted objectives. Docility in supernatural prudence is not so much an acquiescence to the experience of men as to the expectations of God. Caution and circumspection are concerned, not with how much a sacrifice may hurt, but with how much grace the soul has to act. Deliberating upon the norms established by God and determining its action in strict conformity to those rules, the intellect reaches its practical perfection in a human way through supernatural prudence. Then a Catholic not only avoids meat on Friday and assists at Mass on Sunday but sees these and all his working and leisure activity of the remainder of the week as means to his supernatural end. He is the "faithful and prudent servant" (Matt. 24, 45), not the hireling who is neither alert nor interested in supernatural improvement. He is exercising his human talent for practical decision at its very best, as the Apostles did so often in the upper room and elsewhere in their pre-Pentecostal life in Faith.

In a life of Faith the agility of a mind proficient in supernatural prudence is a halting, clumsy stumbling compared to an act of Counsel. By prudence a man brings himself to obey God after deliberation; but in Counsel the Holy Spirit suddenly and without discussion brings the soul into the presence of the Divine Will. In a moment, without a series of serious thoughts, the soul knows exactly what, how, why, when, where, and by what helps the will of God may be fulfilled. The premises for its conclusion are hidden in Divine Wisdom; only the conclusion is revealed to it by Counsel, but its practical action is no less certain. Speculative background may be supplied by the principles of Understanding, the conclusions of Knowledge and the co-ordination of Wisdom, but Counsel alone determines "Let it be so now." In the Gifts which perfect the speculative intellect—Understanding, Knowledge, Wisdom—the mind shares in the eternal, unchanging truths in God.

By Counsel the soul is aware that the Unchanging Will of God is fulfilled amid the changes of the world. It knows that God wills changes without changing His Will, and it conforms to those changes, repeating before each variation or even seeming contradiction: "Let it be so now." Temporary in its context, yet eternal in its significance, each act of Counsel is absolute in one moment and abandoned in the next. The changes willed by the Unchanging Will of God are its only norm; and every human impulse, desire, or judgment to seek security in human deliberation and a slower pace are eliminated as an impertinence to the Holy Spirit. Like a child in its Charity, the soul with Counsel does not ask for a clear realization of every aspect of each situation. It asks only a sign of God's will, a smile of approval or a frown of warning interiorly manifested through the Holy Spirit. The ordinary signs of God's will—His prohibitions, precepts, permissions, exteriorly revealed counsels, or the pattern of his own acts—may be lacking, but Counsel grants an interior assurance in an act of discernment of good from evil, the greater good from the lesser, in each situation which would confound the soul functioning under ordinary prudential judgments.

Counsel from the Holy Spirit is not, however, protestant to external norms, but rather it perfects the soul in understanding and applying them. It nails no theses to a church door nor fills a Tower with the priests of God. It does not divide God against Himself, however much it may separate men among themselves. Counsel does not make God ludicrous to guarantee men liberty.

How human liberty is preserved by Counsel is a mystery of the movement of the Holy Spirit. In the intimate instruction which the Holy Spirit gives to the soul in Counsel, there seems to be no alternative. The Holy Spirit does not engage in arbitration, but asks complete acceptance, since such is the law of grace: "For it is God who works in you, both to will and to accomplish, according to his good will" (Phil. 2, 13). For many, even the apparent encroachment of Counsel upon the cherished dominion of a man over his own act is sufficient reason to deny it entry into the soul, or even into reasonable discussion. They may be the slaves of every kind of habit or the dupes of any kind of deception, but to serve the will of God under inspiration seems repugnant. They will not serve Him whose counsels they have not shared. Because they cannot understand precisely how the Holy Spirit, who fashioned the body of Christ in the womb of the Blessed Virgin Mary, works within the soul to fecundate it with right intentions and judgments, they are militant to defend human liberty at whatever price to divine prerogatives.

For those, on the other hand, who through actual experience of the loving movement of the Holy Spirit, or through theological understanding can know that "God works all in all . . ." (1 Cor.

12, 6), especially in the Gift of Counsel, the dominion of God is preserved without the slightest diminution in the liberty of men. Liberty is something quite different from doubt or even deliberation, which are so much a part of ordinary prudential actions. Indecision and independence are not the characteristics of liberty but, on the contrary, decisiveness and dependence are. Freedom is not a rack full of possibilities but the power and determination to act. A suspended judgment, moreover, is the product of lethargy arising from negligence rather than of true prudence. In surrendering all deliberation to God, the soul with Counsel does not lose its liberty. It gains rather a sureness and determination which repudiate the false elation of pride and the spurious advantages of reconsidering the good and evil of what God has manifestly decided. Knowing the will of God with a certitude inspired by the Spirit of God, the soul has no need of a more humanly acceptable explanation to assure it that in Counsel the soul is both pre-eminently free and prudent.

Counsel does not recollect the past but recognizes it in the present. The laborious process of bringing facts and principles from the back of one's head to the forefront of one's consciousness is one of the limitations of prudence, not one of its perfections. The human mind ordinarily has to pause to recall the past, no matter how trigger-quick its memory may be. In Counsel the entire picture of the present is framed in the past, and the soul sees the whole at a single glance. At once it sees the basis of all supernatural merit in the abundantly sufficient redemptive and satisfactory Passion and Death of Christ. Between the Cross and the crucial moment in which Counsel acts, some meritorious action of the soul itself must have taken place, since Counsel is present only in souls in the state of grace. On the basis of Christ's merits and its own, the soul has a living Hope, formed by Charity and leading to eternal life. That Hope brings the past into the present and is associated with Counsel in its eminently prudent act.

Counsel's judgment of the present, moreover, is especially clear.

The soul is constantly reminded by the Holy Spirit: "Behold, now is the acceptable time; behold, now is the day of salvation" (2 Cor. 6, 2). When the Gift of Counsel acts, the significance of the moment cannot be lost, since the soul is aware that it must fulfill the will of God completely or fail to comply with it at all. When the will of God is manifested interiorly, even if no exterior obligation or law binds it, the soul finds itself with the choice of either serving God or sinning. Yet the soul is not told what to do and then left without further assistance from the Holy Spirit. It is also instructed concerning the immediate circumstances of its act and any possible impediments. Peter, although prudence would tell him that "it is not permissible for a Jew to associate with a foreigner or to visit him . . . making no doubt . . . came" (Acts 10, 28f.) to Cornelius, so that "the grace of the Holy Spirit was poured out upon the Gentiles also" (Acts 10, 45).

In both Peter and Cornelius the obstacles of natural repugnance or supernatural incongruity were dispelled. In every act of Counsel the soul is instructed what precautions to take and what obstacles to avoid. Joan of Arc had a Counsel within her own soul which was far more practical than the councils of her enemies. Her precautions of purity and prayer before the triumph at Orleans were obviously more farseeing than the preparations of those who permitted licentiousness and blasphemies as practical necessities in military life. Such decisions had not previously been made, but in her soul the Holy Spirit commanded: "Let it be so now." When, moreover, her national victory brought her to personal defeat and her taking up the sword for justice drove her to a flaming stake of martyrdom, the Holy Spirit again spoke softly within her: "Let it be so now," since "the sufferings of this time are not worthy to be compared with the glory to come" (Rom. 8, 18).

"The glory to come" is the consistent motivation of the act of Counsel, even though the inspiration of that Gift may not be a constant factor of any Christian's life. No one may expect that he can enjoy an entire lifetime, or even a long period of time, in a vacation from deliberation and the labors of prudence because of Counsel. Besides occasional acts which are venially sinful, and in which no virtue is employed even if none is destroyed, the most elevated souls have to walk their own way and form their own prudent judgments. The activity of Counsel may be quite frequent, but it is not constant, since the Spirit breathes where He wills. When, however, Counsel does act, it is alway consistent in seeking the "glory that is to come."

In getting the meritorious most out of life, Counsel is a true perfection of the practical intellect. It provides the soul with a selective constancy that is both artistic and instinctive. The right word, the correct act, the proper restraint, or the fearless insistence on salvation, are part of the protocol in which Counsel is adept. For the rules of its judgments, Counsel looks to Understanding, Knowledge, and Wisdom, but its own artistry consists in adapting and applying the general norms to particular situations. Its instantaneous and intense certitude seem almost instinctive. The movement of Counsel is like that of the much maligned butterfly, whose way seems inconsistent to intellectual and spiritual caterpillars who hunch along with their feet—and their faces—on the ground of human prudence. To human prudence the acts of Counsel seem impulsive, but to the one inspired, any delay in analyzing the dictates of the Holy Spirit would be a failure to obey God, "Who worketh all things according to the counsel of his will" (Ephes. 1, 11).

In fulfilling the will of God, Counsel is vigorous as well as vigilant. If it receives dictates, it gives directives. From Understanding, Knowledge, and Wisdom under the Holy Spirit it accepts norms; and to Piety, Fortitude, and Fear it gives explicit directions. Like Prudence, Counsel is the hinge of the cardinal factors of moral life. In the commerce between ends and means, Counsel makes the exchange. It knows what to do or to avoid, to say or to suppress, to pursue or to abandon. It knows both when not to "strive against the stream of the river" or "even unto death fight for justice" (Ecclus. 4, 32-3). Its direction enables Piety, Fortitude, and Fear to act with dignity and decisiveness, so that Divine Gifts need not depend upon the human norms of prudence to guide them.

The whole-hearted enthusiasm and religious eagerness of Piety need Counsel, so that the soul may be intoxicated with devotion before God and sober among men. What, moreover, is allowable for an adopted member of the divine family is regulated by Counsel, which rules out of devotion anything that is fanciful or fanatical. In all the works of justice which Piety inspires, Counsel provides instruction concerning the best means "of sharing in the ministry that is in behalf of the saints" (2 Cor. 8, 4).

Any share in the ministry requires the strength of Fortitude, and consequently the control of Counsel. Fortitude would be a reckless daring if Counsel did not determine that in the circumstances the extreme is the middle ground of virtue. Counsel makes of a strong man a Simon of Cyrene, and of a weak woman an Agatha or an Agnes. For one, strength is in the silent acceptance of a Cross. For another, it is a fearless proclamation of purity before a tyrant. For both, Fortitude is the fulfilling of the will of God under the guidance of Counsel.

The impulses Counsel restrains in Fortitude it stimulates in Fear. Counsel fosters in Fear a horror of sin without allowing it the single-eyed terror of the doomed. It always modifies repentance with Hope. Yet Counsel indicates that filial respect demands the suppression of presumption, so that not the slightest irreverence for holy things may enter into a soul in which Fear has begun to be wise. Counsel further instructs Fear how temporal goods should be used as instruments of an ever-increasing Charity, so that this use may complete the soul's renunciation, and bring about its naked following of Christ.

Through its direction of the Gifts of Piety, Fortitude, and Fear, Counsel evidences its practical perfection. Knowledge of concrete things is imperfect unless it is extended from principles to particulars. God's knowledge, because it is perfect, extends to particulars; human knowledge becomes perfect by extending to particulars. God acts without restraint, men with a struggle. In the effort to know all the particular details that are involved in a human action, even under the impetus of Piety, Fortitude, or Fear, the soul shares something of divine knowledge through Counsel. Like the Word of God which it reflects, Counsel is "living and effective and more piercing than any two-edged sword; and reaching unto the division of the soul and the spirit, of joints also and the marrow, and is a discerner of the thoughts and intents of the heart" (Heb. 4, 12). Since the Gifts of the Holy Spirit are for a soul's sanctification rather than for society, the discernment and division is within the soul itself, its own motives and methods, its judgment of its end and means. The life, efficiency, keenness, and extension of Counsel are, moreover, not limited to acts performed under Piety, Fortitude, and Fear. They extend to all good works in which the Holy Spirit supplies the practical judgment to assist another or to accept his aid, to advise or to seek advice.

Either in being docile to others or in directing them, Counsel is active. Its action within the practical intellect is always a willing receptivity, in which nothing comes from human judgment but nothing goes against it. Since the soul with Counsel is aware not only of what has been said but of Who has spoken, all doubt is removed, even if many difficulties remain. Even when the still, small voice of the Spirit within the soul impels it to seek the advice of one of God's human instruments, the soul first forms a judgment that accepting advice is its most acceptable activity. A blind Paul was given only one step in the process of his becoming the light of the Gentiles: "Arise and go into the city, and there it will be told you what you should do" (Acts 7, 7). He prepared for the most active apostolate by complete docility. He was not instructed to seek out Ananias but to wait. In the city Ananias, despite his own well-founded prudential misgivings, restored sight and supernatural life to Paul, although he perhaps never knew during his lifetime the good he had done, and his whole career reached its climax in an act he did not fully understand. Rarely does the Holy Spirit so inspire a soul that it does not have to "go into the city" by communicating with others, who are not needed to verify the inspiration but to validate its usefulness in the soul's salvation or the social life of Christians. Never does the Holy Spirit so inspire a soul that its practical judgment runs counter to the ultimate and absolute decision of Christ's Church. Cornelius was submissive to the authority of the Holy Spirit and to that of the infant Church, and, although he had been visited by an angel and had received direct revelations, the Holy Spirit instructed him through an angel to "send and fetch Simon who is surnamed Peter" (Acts 10, 5). In all who receive the Spirit of Counsel there is the assurance that they should seek Peter in his successors and their subordinates in the administration of the Church.

Whenever, therefore, a soul is truly docile to the Holy Spirit, it is likewise tractable to the determinations of the Church. Many holy men and women without hierarchical rank have admonished others, among them churchmen, to perform works pleasing to God. St. Bernard, St. Bridget, St. Francis of Paula, and St. Vincent Ferrer have given edifying and exacting instructions to others. Yet even these advisers, who have the affidavits of their own sanctity, have submitted to the scrutiny of those less holy but in greater authority in the Church. St. Catherine of Siena, in summoning the Vicar of Christ to return to Rome, advised him strenuously in the spirit of the Counsel she had received, yet at the same time she submitted her conduct and her judgment to the correction of the same Shepherd of

Christendom. Her faithful and fearless reformation and restoration of Papal dignity, in contrast to later revolts of protest, had the security and submissiveness which are the seal of divine inspiration. The interior inspiration and impulse to "let it be so now" is dependent upon the permission of exterior authority, and both are under the guidance of the Holy Spirit.

The workings of the Gift of Counsel, in accepting or offering advice, are more obvious in the difficult decisions of the Christian life, but they need not be absent from even the easiest. When, for example, human prudence would warn against it and supernatural prudence would not command it, Counsel may insist with unanswerable urgency upon the fulfillment of the evangelical counsels under the vows of a religious. Those who hear the call cannot always explain it intelligibly, but they have no doubt that they must arise, go into a community, where it will be told them what they should do to save their souls. They have in their possession a pearl more precious to them than wealth; in their blood is an impulse more imperious than concupiscence, and in their hearts there is a command that dominates even their self-love, as yet unruly. In the poverty, chastity, and obedience of religious life, which human prudence finds extreme, Counsel assures the soul of a way to life everlasting, despite obstacles and disappointments. Nor does Counsel abandon a daughter who for a time or a lifetime sacrifices her own preferences to assist a parent who needs her. Nor is Counsel exercised exclusively in abstinence and abnegation. A person about to be married may have an interior supernatural conviction that in the sacrament of Matrimony is the source of his salvation. Another inheriting wealth may be moved to distribute it to the poor and go away happy, following Christ. A mother about to have a child to the astonishment and perhaps annoyance of contrary medical opinion, or a man adhering to a just contract despite avoidable personal loss, may both be inspired by the Holy Spirit to do an ordinary thing extraordinarily well.

The effects of Counsel may, moreover, be almost completely interior. Even in the most ordinary actions, souls of various temperaments may require distinctive and instantaneous advice such as their own prudential judgments cannot supply. A person who has a quick and lasting reaction to every situation and stimulant may need the inspiration of Counsel merely to hold his tongue. Later he will marvel at the action as much because it is so out-of-character as because it kept him from blundering. Counsel, moreover, can provide a constant encouragement to those whose reaction is slow but lasting, and who tend to lose hope because they consider more their own failure than the mercy of God. Counsel keeps from their minds that last straw, a little thing to be sure, but an overwhelming load to the melancholic. To the sanguine, who are "children tossed to and fro, and carried about with every wind of doctrine by the wickedness of men" (Ephes. 4, 14), Counsel gives an intimate pedagogy in consistency. It schools such souls not with a rod but with the Cross, and it measures out at opportune times both consolations and contradictions. For those who drawl their concepts and dawdle through their lives, Counsel has a cogent command to be not only hearers of the word but doers also. To each person and for every changing mood, Counsel has an appropriate inspiration which can overcome natural inclinations and foster obedience to God's will.

In obeying God and overcoming themselves, Christians open their hearts to others. As the sons of God they are instructed to "Be merciful, as your heavenly Father also is merciful" (Luke 6, 36); in fulfilling that command, they attain their own happiness, since "blessed are the merciful, for they shall obtain mercy" (Matt. 5, 7). The command and the consolation of mercy are intimately connected in the teaching of Christ and the inspiration of the Holy Spirit. Mercy comes first from God to the soul, which then returns to God through its merciful acts toward others. From Charity, mercy derives its force, and from Counsel, its direction. Charity inclines the soul to overcome self-love and to stop whining about its own miseries, so that it can adopt the afflictions of others as its own. Through Charity men become like Christ, and less like Cain; they are their brother's keepers, not their killers, at least through indifference and neglect. They actively and affectionately bear the burdens of one another and thus fulfill the law of Christ (Gal. 6, 2). They unashamedly "weep with them that weep" (Rom. 12, 15), and they repudiate completely the cynicism which protests that being merciful is asking for trouble. They are aware, on the contrary, that they are avoiding troubles by obtaining mercy from God. Their Charity moves them to share with others the good things they have, and Counsel is their almoner.

In distributing the alms granted by Charity, Counsel directs both corporal and spiritual works of mercy. Because its judgment is practical, it is not bewildered by spiritual or physical evil, since it knows both good and evil in a divine context. Some of the spiritual works which Counsel directs are within the secrecy of a man's soul. When and how he should forgive offenses, bear injuries patiently, or pray for the living and the dead, especially his persecutors, a man learns from the Holy Spirit through Counsel. That same Gift directs him in spiritual actions which involve the intellectual and moral lives of others. He instructs the ignorant or advises the doubtful, "not in the persuasive words of human wisdom, but in showing of the Spirit and power" (1 Cor. 2, 4) He consoles the afflicted and gives fraternal correction to sinners in the way Christ Himself advised— "between thee and him alone" (Matt. 18, 15).

No less appropriate to Charity nor less subordinate to Counsel, the corporal works of mercy are meritorious means for the soul to perfect itself in benefiting others. In some cases a person merely gives away external goods: food to the hungry, drink to the thirsty, clothing and hospitality to those in need; yet each of these acts may be expressive of an intense Charity and the control of Counsel. At times mercy demands more. To visit the sick or those in prison, to redeem captives or the victims of injustice, to bury the dead, are all actions which exact from the soul a continual exercise of Charity and the inspiration of Counsel.

In being merciful the soul is blessed by obtaining mercy, which is the basis for Hope and the background for every future act under Counsel. Mercy has, moreover, a pervasive influence in a person's life, producing fruits in his Christian personality. The fruits appropriate to the merciful acts, not the prudential judgments in which Counsel gives directions, are goodness and kindness (cf. Gal. 5, 22). Goodness is characteristic of a soul practised in prudential judgments and in the exercise of every virtue which purges out self-love. It is as austere as ivory and as virginal. To anyone seeking advice or aid, goodness is a sign of an impartial judge and a selfless handmaid. Kindness, on the other hand, adds to the virginal purity of goodness a maternally warm attractiveness. Kindness has the countenance of a nursing mother, content with whatever small contribution it can make to sustain life and relieve need. In kindness there is tender human sentiment without anything sentimental. There is an approximation of the benignity of God, who "is kind to the unthankful, and to the evil" (Luke 6, 35). At Cana and on Calvary goodness and kindness were together in the soul of the Virgin Mother of God, who relieved the embarrassment of servants or accepted from the open side of her Son an infant Church to be nursed by her loving counsels. She who had said "Be it done to me according to thy word" (Luke 1, 38) taught the Church not to fear but to keep faith with the will of God, who had promised: "My counsel shall stand, and all my will shall be done" (Isaias 46, 10).

More to educate themselves than to produce external results, Christians have repeated as a petition what God proclaimed as a promise. They pray: "Thy will be done on earth as it is in heaven" (Matt. 6, 10), and evidence their docility to the Holy Spirit. In this the soul has its share of omnipotence; it conforms to the will of Almighty God. What Adam could not accomplish by insubordination or Satan by defiance, the simplest soul does by co-operating in God's governance of the universe by its prayers. If the souls in heaven do not ask God for proof that their happiness will be eternal, the soul with Counsel does not demand to know exactly how its acts fit into the pattern of Divine Providence. In judging particular truths, the soul desires only the will of God, and its holy practicality is not concerned with the possibilities of human misunderstanding or even pharisaical scandals. Its petition "Thy will be done" expresses its acceptance totally, lovingly, unhesitatingly, unashamedly without human deliberation, of the moment-to-moment advice of Counsel: "Let it be so now."

The acceptable now, the day of salvation, is Counsel's sudden illumination of life's most serious thought. When Counsel acts, life can never be humdrum. Yet Counsel does not specialize in spectacular action to satisfy glamor-starved souls with religious interests. Even in a life apparently most ordinary, Counsel guides the soul and gives it the easy motion of a practised athlete, with no breathless bursts of uncontrolled spiritual activity. It eliminates all scruples by its quiet assurance, but it also makes the conscience all the more tender. Aware of evil and its own inheritance from Adam, the soul redeemed by Christ prays that the will of God may be done, and that it may know its own role, however great or small, however active or passive. An act of Counsel answers that petition by enlightening the practical judgment, restraining curiosity about consequences, and confirming the soul's conviction to fulfill the will of God, to "let it be so now."

Counsel

(*Summary from the* Summa)

"... in the seeking of counsel, man needs to be directed by God, who comprehends all things, and this is done through the Gift of Counsel, by which a man is directed as though counseled by God, just as in human affairs those who are unable to take counsel for themselves seek counsel from those who are wiser. . . . The Gift of Counsel is appropriate to the children of God inasmuch as the reason is instructed by the Holy Spirit concerning what we should do. . . . The human mind, by the very fact that it is directed by the Holy Spirit, is enabled to direct itself and others.

"Counsel considered as a Gift of the Holy Spirit guides us in all things which are ordered to the end of eternal life, whether they are necessary for salvation or not. . . ."

—*Second of the Second Part, question fifty-two,* passim.

VI
Family Likeness
The Gift of Piety

Family Likeness

There is an easy competence for family life in every one of us. After all, we were made to live in a home and are as wisely equipped for such life by the divine Architect as fish are for life in water or birds for flight through the air. We like the looks of those at home because, as a matter of fact, they look like us; we can understand their gifts and deficiencies, for by blood we share with them the common source of both. Disinterested love needs no protestations here, for it is the atmosphere which allows the family to breathe and live. We can relax and be ourselves within the family; here there is no need for armor, nothing to be gained by bluff, no mercy for swank, and no scorn for weakness. We move through that family life with none of the timidity and caution of the advance made to strangers, none of the haunting fear that eats into our confidence as we go forth into strange lands or into levels of society that are new to us. We are at home, and our every movement shows it: here we are seen at our very best and at our very worst; for here we are at home. We belong.

This easy competence of ours is strictly limited to human family life, for it is only within those strict limits that we are natural sons. The divine family is altogether out of our orbit; there is nothing in our nature that gives us the privilege of calling God our Father. It is only when the supernatural has loosed its breathless powers into our lives that we can be called sons of God; even that power exceeding all nature does not change our nature but, leaving it intact, elevates it. We are still not sons of God except by adoption.

It is well for us to understand how far God had to go in this matter of adoption so that we may not hesitate to believe how far He invites us to go. Adoption, as we ordinarily understand it, demands no more than warm mercy that throws open the doors of home to a homeless child, giving the child access not merely to the hearth but to the very hearts of the household; granted the continuance of mercy's delicate graciousness, the adopted child is immediately and forever one of the family. Knowing our own powers, we do not attempt to adopt any being not of our nature; the best efforts of the most mawkishly sentimental fall short of making a dog one of the family. If we could so elevate the nature of the dog that he would become like ourselves, knowing and loving as we do, speaking our speech, cultivating our manners, aiming at our goals, undetectable as a stranger while he moves through the complexities of human social living, then we would have some little idea of what we expect of God in His adoption of us as sons. There would, in fact, be much less of distance bridged in a dog's leap to human heights than in the soaring flight of man or woman to the divine heights of God's own family. There is infinity between our nature and God's, between our life and His; and we have absolutely no equipment for divine living.

The adoption by which we become sons of God is obviously a work possible only to omnipotence; nothing else could possibly overcome the difficulties involved in such adoption. If we are to live the divine family life as sons, we must share in the divine life; we must be given a life, over and above our human one, that will enable us to live on a divine plane. Omnipotence overcomes this difficulty by the gift of sanctifying grace; by this gift we are divinely alive, by its absence we are supernaturally dead. If omnipotence were to stop short at the gift of the life of grace, we would be supernatural paralytics incapable of the least activity; a poor kind of adoption indeed, and a meagre share of the family life into which we are adopted. That we might be able to act divinely, omnipotence elevates our every active capacity by the infusion, along with grace, of divinely perfect virtues; the supreme virtue thus divinely given is Charity, which thus becomes the source of all this divine movement, sharing its goal of divine movement by directing all the other virtues, and forging the bond by which we are one with God.

With Charity as the bond of union, with the virtues moving under the direction of Charity to the goal that is properly God's, we can and do move on the family plane of the divine. But we do it badly. We are dead without grace, utterly inactive without the virtues; with no more than grace and the virtues, we are clumsy, awkward, falling far short of the routine activity of this family into which we have been adopted. Even though our human limitations are divinely extended by the infused virtues, they are still limitations that do not make for ease or competence in the divine family; the virtues, for all their divine perfection, still work in the human manner, making their way laboriously up to principles, lumbering, sliding, slipping down from the principles to their application, waiting on reason's cautious and uncertain investigations, harassed by the sallies of ignorance and passion, accomplishing their goals only at the cost of mighty effort. We have more reason for feeling out of place than a dog at a banquet table; we have none of the divine social graces. All about us is swift, sure knowledge; love that thrusts home to its target as sharply as a bolt of lightning; and actions untrammeled by indecision, caution, or the sheer drag of time.

We are embarrassed in the divinely civilized social life proper to God; and we are an embarrassment to the divine family which has adopted us. We are infinitely out of our element, as red-necked, heavy-handed, and ill-at-ease as a thug in a convent. We need something more than that participation of divine life which is grace, something more than those divinely elevated powers of action which are the virtues; something that will fit us to move as God moves socially, a help that will make our souls easily responsive to God's own movement through our faculties and the divinely given virtues. That social gift by which we act as God acts in all His relations with others is the gift of the Holy Ghost which is called the Gift of Piety.

"Now the Holy Ghost moves us to this effect among others, of having a filial affection towards God, according to Romans 8, 15: 'You have received the spirit of adoption of sons, whereby we cry: Abba (Father).' And since it belongs properly to piety to pay duty and worship to one's father, it follows that piety, whereby, at the Holy Ghost's instigation, we pay worship and duty to God as our Father, is a gift of the Holy Ghost."[1] This is the gift which completes and perfects our adoption into the family of God. Because of this gift, it can be said of us: like father, like son. With it, it is not only true that we live with a divine life, act towards divine goals, but we also act divinely; for by this gift we share the justice of God.

That note of justice is fundamental. The Gift of Piety deals only with our relations to others, and with all our relations with others. In other words, it deals with the proper field of justice, perfecting the virtue of justice to its fullest divine bloom. Just as justice is the absolute requisite for social living among men, so the Gift of Piety is the absolute requisite for the social living of the sons of God. On the purely human level, it is not good for man to be alone. He needs society both because of his insufficiency and because of his superabundance. To obtain the goods that make for full human life, men must pool their efforts, no man is sufficient unto himself; and the same is true as regards the warding off of the evils and dangers that threaten the fullness of human living. For the most part, this pooling of effort for good and against evil does not make heroic demands on individual men; its stuff is little things—routine, common, domestic—for justice is an integral part of every man's every day, not the soaring, infrequent moments of heroism. On the side of superabundance, we need social life in order that we might share the

[1] St. Thomas, *Summa theol.*, IIa IIae, q. 121, a. 1.

riches that are ours, for we are made in the image of God, the perfect agent, who can act only to share of His bounty. We are most perfectly in His image when we are distributing to others the things that cannot be lost in the sharing. We need others to give them of our truth, to teach them; we need others to give them of our goodness, to love them; we need others to minister to their misery, to give them mercy. We need others, not merely that we might through them come home to God but that we might bring God home to them in our mirroring of the generosity of divine actions.

We can, of course, abuse society, making the lives of others mere adjuncts, subsidiary possessions of our own; and thereby suffer the ultimate loneliness that is the inevitable fruit of injustice. In our time, injustice, the guaranteed destruction of social life, needs no spelling out: we need only write plundering satiety for assistance given and received, panicky flight from the misery of others for mercy, perversion of truth and abuse of the good, or, in milder form, a cautiously selfish denial to others of the truth and goodness that is our own. To all appearances injustice merely takes advantage of the fact of social life; in reality, it corrodes the very foundation of men's life together. It is directly to our purpose here to note a peculiarly subtle danger to an age like our own where injustice flourishes. In the desperate struggle to keep a spark of human social life in a society almost fatally infected by the disease of injustice, in the crucial battle to maintain the bare minimum of justice whose absence is death, it is not hard to overlook entirely the divine perfection of human social life, the vigorous health of a social life far beyond our own which is the routine effect of omnipotence working within the souls of men and women with whom we live. The threats to the family life of men may distract us from the glory of the social life of God shared by men, by ordinary men, by men like ourselves and in this day and age. We must not forget that we are now sons of God because so many men are afraid to live up to their humanity;

we must not be blind to our family life with God just because the family life of men is disfigured by disease.

The infused virtue of justice banishes injustice to the outer regions, making our will prompt and eager to give others their due; the infused virtue of mercy bubbles over into the lives of others in a steady flow of gratuitous gifts to all those to whom we are in some way bound, even though the bond be no sturdier than this other's present need. The Gift of Piety, by which we are at home even in the family life of God, makes us fiercely just, valiantly defending champions of others rather than their plunderers, afire, athirst for justice; it makes us merciful in the broad, uncounting measure of God's own thoughtfulness, ministering with an instinctive sympathy and appreciation to every need, wherever found. It is significant that St. Thomas stresses the homely character of Piety in his insistence that it deals only with common things, the ordinary, in contrast to the gifts of Counsel and Fortitude with their concentration on the very difficult. A moment's consideration makes plain that this is not nearly so much a restriction of the field of the Gift of Piety as a profound tribute to its perfection of social life; for it means that by the touch of the Gift of Piety, all things become homely, common, because they all become domestic, details in the family life of God, with the world seen as no more than a spare room of God's house pressed into temporary service for the pilgrim children on their way home. Inevitably, Piety leads men to the full fruits of social living: those who thirst after justice shall be filled, those who are merciful shall obtain mercy.

The principal object of the Gift of Piety is God as Father, and all things that pertain to God as Father: ourselves and other men as His children, all other creatures as His domestic possessions. We can, then, get some appreciation of this gift of the Holy Ghost by considering its effect on our family life with God, with men, and in the world.

FAMILY LIKENESS

The perfection of our family life with God through the Gift of Piety can be seen, at least in silhouette fashion, by considering a son's regard for such a Father, a son's appreciation of this divine Father, and the consequent outlook of the son of such a Father. It is true that other virtues look to God, but not precisely as to a Father. The virtue of religion, for example, and the Gift of Fear of the Lord both concentrate on the divine excellence and flood our hearts with humility and reverential worship. Charity has eyes only for the divine goodness and rushes to embrace the divine friend. The Gift of Piety looks to God as to a Father, and puts the filial touch in all of our actions, all of our thoughts, all of our dealings with others. By it, under the movement of the Holy Ghost, we focus on the paternal benignity of God.

It is unfortunate that the word "benign" has been disemboweled in modern usage. It does imply the absence of harshness, a total estrangement from brutality, but that is no excuse for identifying it with futility; the good-hearted failure whose gentle smile and kindly eyes argue that he means well but at the same time guarantee that he is too soft, too often beaten, to help anyone—such a man is not benign. He might like to be; but benignity is made of much sterner stuff. To St. Thomas, "the benign are those whom a splendid fire of love has burning to do good to others." To be caught up in the consideration of the paternal benignity of God, then, means to look at God's fatherly activity, at His kindly will, His farseeing providence, the tireless care which embraces our every sleeping and waking moment, the patience without limit, the forbearance that cannot be worn thin by our perversity, the understanding that knows our hearts better than we do ourselves.

To say all this is to say no more than that we are sons looking at our father's works precisely as our father's. Every child cherishes the illusion of the utter perfection of its human father. This man, this father, is so much bigger than the child, so much stronger, so much wiser; it is easy for the child, and almost inevitable, to conclude that its father knows all answers, can do all things, understands every problem and will come to the rescue in every crisis and against every mistake. We smile, remembering this illusion of our own childhood, reflecting on the inevitable shattering of the child's happy mistake by the unrelenting blows of time. Eventually the child will know the human limitations of its parents, and its reverential admiration will too often be replaced by a superior pity which is understandable in the light of youth's quick strength, high hopes, and long dreams but which is no less false than the original hero worship. Yet in a deeper sense, the child's estimate of its father is more a reflection of divine truths than an empty illusion. This parent is the principle from which flows the life of the child, but the principle only under God; he is a blurred image of the divine paternity, a secondary cause whose every moment of causality rests on and is explained by the supporting power and action of the First Cause. There *is* an omnipotent and omniscient Father of every child born into the world. That sublime truth comes to life in the details of our daily living through the Gift of Piety; by it, our mature eyes open to the truth that childhood's simplicity took so for granted, and it is precisely in seeing our eternally enduring childhood in the family of God that the veils are torn away from the flaming benignity of God our Father.

We begin then to appreciate the Father of this divine family into which we have been adopted. From this aspect, the Gift of Piety gives a divine perfection to that part of justice which is the virtue of religion; under the Gift of Piety, religion has an altogether new flavor and a mode of action far surpassing the human step-by-step procedure. The virtue of religion, looking to the divine majesty and the abyss that lies between the finite and the Infinite, demands that we acknowledge our place in the universe under God. It commands that we admit that God is the first source of our being, and that we give

Him the respect and worship due to the Creator from His creature.

Perfected by the Gift of Piety, this activity of religion becomes a family affair; not so much a duty which can be proved to the hilt by careful reasoning, an obligation that holds rigidly, however reluctant our heart, our hands, and our feet. It is rather the child's boastful pride, eager praise, stout defense, and whole-hearted loyalty. We insist on the subordination of sonship precisely because this gives us a claim to such a Father, in sharp contrast to the modern's sullen resentment against or rejection of God as a rival superior to man and challenging man's supremacy. We are not jealous of God's perfection, not resentful, rebellious, sullen, mocking or scornful in protest against the sublime perfection of God. This is a family affair. He is our Father, we are His sons, and extremely proud of the relationship. We are delighted that He is so superior, and shout His praises to the corners of the earth. The demands of religion are met, then, by spontaneous rushes of the heart to get more done, and more quickly, than any obligation could demand.

In concrete terms, we readily bow before His holy words in Sacred Scripture. Whether we fully understand them or not, these are the words of our Father, a heritage of wisdom untainted by any falsity; so they carry an authority that reverberates through our whole being, an authority that is answered by a reverent honor quicker than an echo. These are words to be savored, repeated, mulled over, penetrated; and always with gratitude welling within us to the Father who has told us so much of truth beyond our powers. It is our prompt pleasure to give all honor to the Blessed Mother of God, to the creature who was closer than any other to our Father. The saints, those men and women whose whole lives were vivid testimony to their love and loyalty to our Father, are the objects of our special affection and close comradeship. This is a family affair.

As a result of Piety's perfection of religion, all the acts of this virtue will have a divine air about them, and that divine promptness, the common mark of the Gifts of the Holy Ghost, which leaves our human way so far behind. Thus, for example, devotion, which is the first act of religion, is a prompt will to serve the majestic Creator of the universe. With the divine domestic note injected into this service, we must look to our own human family living for an appreciation of the perfection of this prompt service, for now it is the child's service, not the labors of a servant. Our devotion finds a vague parallel in the small child's eager pride and grateful sense of privilege the first time it is allowed a share, even though it be only a token share, in the adult labors of its parents: the tiny girl's busy wielding of a dust cloth for the first time, the toddling boy's momentary maturity as he is allowed to hold a tool or spend an hour in his father's shop. True, the children soon tire of this privilege of partnership because they soon understand there are more important, more enticing things to do. But the sons of God never find more important or enticing things to do than to serve that omnipotent Father. Some few, through the kindness of God and the generosity of men, will be able to give service utterly to that divine family; and this is religious or priestly vocation seen in its very roots. Of course this vocation is impossible to men because it dedicates a man or woman to moving divinely in the divine family circle for every moment of a lifetime; such a vocation is a divine social grace given to men to make spontaneous this gesture of complete service to the Father.

The act of the virtue of religion which is called adoration has us bend down before the Creator in acknowledgment of the absolute sovereignty of the Lord and Master of all things. The Gift of Piety makes adoration practically a state of mind. Adoration thus perfected is not only the child's big-eyed wonder at paternal genius, it is the adult son's penetration of fatherly benignity and so of fatherly excellence. We are never out of reminders of that paternal sovereignty for every detail of our lives and of the lives with which we come into contact, every item of the world in which we live shouts a story of that omnipotent paternal care. It is not without significance that this Gift of Piety, perfecting the will, is directed by the intellectual gift of Knowledge, the gift which comes to the divine through creatures. All the world is a record of fatherly perfection and thoughtfulness; we read it avidly, treasuring every detail lovingly; and, having read, we adore, adore with all our mind, all our heart, all our soul, this wondrous sovereignty of Him who is our Father.

By sacrifice, the virtue of religion gives public and sensible acknowledgment of the supreme sovereignty of God and thus furnishes an outlet for the adoration and devotion which is crowding our hearts. Perfected by the Gift of Piety, sacrifice is no longer merely a duty to which obligation drives us. The Mass, parish services, the opportunities for community expression of our dependence on the Creator are family triumphs, intimately personal achievements celebrated by the family, public glorification of the name of that family into which adoption has admitted us. The Catholic's serious obligation to hear Mass on Sunday is by no means the whole explanation of churches crowded despite bitter cold, stifling heat, or driving rains. We insist on having our part in these family affairs, and only very serious barriers can keep us from them.

Under the Gift of Piety, religion's act of prayer becomes the talk of home. Often enough it is small talk; the friendly buzz that apparently has no momentous consequence, merely making the music of a home. Sometimes it is courageous, gallant, even sublime. Sometimes it is shamefaced, humiliating, apologetic, or pleading in the name of helplessness. At all times, it is a family affair to which we move divinely, as sons of God should; keen to its privileges, exultant in its companionship, proud of its praises. The wonder is that not all prayer is in song.

The attitudes and outlook of the members of a family are never locked up within the walls of a home as though they were disgraceful family secrets. They are carried to the world, and proudly. Inevitably, then, the adopted son of God developes a special, a divine, outlook as a result of his awareness of the flaming benignity of his Father and his appreciation of the perfection of that Father. If an outlook is hard to define, at least it is easy to identify; certainly it is determined by the thing we most concentrate on and for which we have the sharpest appreciation. It is in terms of this that we think first, this is what flavors our judgments, this is the special color of all our thoughts. Husband and wife think first in terms of the family, a medical man in terms of health and disease, an engineer in terms of strains and stresses, and so on. The Gift of Piety gives us a special outlook precisely as sons of God, as members of the divine family; this is the flavor of our judgments, the color of our thoughts.

It can be detected most immediately, and with fundamental implications that reach to the inmost depths of social life, in our attitude towards authority. It is so easy to see the subordination which is authority's correlative as an affront to human dignity, an unwarranted restriction on a man's activity, and a reflection on his adult ability to take care of himself. It can, in other words, be seen as the subjection imposed unjustly on the slave, and maintained only by the constant threat of violence. In this light, certainly subordination is a degrading, disintegrating injustice to a man; and the authority that imposes it is rightly seen as man's enemy. The truth of that matter is that the subordination imposed by rightful authority has an innate nobility all its own. It is a tribute to truth and order; an affirmation of a man's dignity; and a steady nourishment to his strength. This subordination is no less than an insistence on a man's rightful place, a recognition of what is above him and what is below him; it is a protection to a man against making a fool of himself by trying to play god or a beast of himself as he cowers before the burdens of his humanity. The virtues of subordination protect and develop this ennobling subordination in us. Perfected by the Gift of Piety, these virtues look to all holders of authority in the light of the divine paternity, the divine principality which is their source. This is authority's only claim to respect, that it shares the principality of the source of all being; because in some little way, parents, country, superiors are, under God, sources of our being, they lay valid claim to our subjection and obedience. The filial outlook of an adopted son of God sees all these superiors as sharers in the paternal benignity which has so won his heart in the family which has adopted him. His subordination to and respect for his parents becomes a prompt, proud, eager thing. He cannot be a parasite on his country, a glutton for its nourishment and a shirker of its burdens and dangers; he is a patriot because God is his Father and his country has shared in that paternity. To those over him by reason of authority, his subjection is not sullen, resentful, a minimum service given for fear of a whip; for these have authority only because it was given them by God, only because they share the divine paternity. He gives a hardly less eager subjection to those who are above him by reason of learning or sanctity. So it is particularly dear to his heart to honor the saints, a joyous duty that will endure for all of eternity; it will be his special privilege to give the utmost of honor and subordination of the greatest of the saints, Our Lady, the Mother of God.

A second, and even more far-reaching, characteristic of this adopted son's outlook will be a detailed program of action towards other men and the world, a program patterned on that of his divine Father. The importance of this, and its extreme extensiveness, demand that it be given treatment under a heading of its own.

The Gift of Piety completes our adoption into the divine family, and thereby gives us a son's regard for our heavenly Father and an adopted divine son's outlook. Its effect, then, on our life with men is a divinization of our social life. For an exhaustive statement of this effect, which must have omnipotence at its source, we would have to trace the divinely sublime perfection of legal, distributive, and commutative justice in all their complex and far-flung details from the purely private workings of a gratuitous promise through all the complexities of legislative and judicial activity to the worldwide interrelations of nations; to complete the picture, it would be necessary to see the divine perfection of the social virtues like gratitude, veracity, affability, liberality, as well as mercy and meekness. It is by this array of virtues that men work out their lives together; it is by the divine infusion of virtues to match these natural ones that men live their social life on a supernatural level; the perfection of these supernatural virtues by the Gift of Piety allows men to live their social life divinely. It must be insisted that this ultimate perfection of social life is not a rare thing reserved for a few heroic souls. The Gifts of the Holy Ghost are given to every soul in the state of grace, to every soul free of mortal sin; moreover, their operation is a necessity for salvation. We conclude, then, to the stupendous truth that this divinization of our social life is as common a thing as that share of divine life which is sanctifying grace; men and women all about us are living social life divinely, and so routinely as to allow us to take it for granted, thus becoming blind to one of the wonders that omnipotence has worked among men. This inspiring truth can be confirmed, and the divinization of our social life seen graphically and simply, by a meditative glance at the models of that living that have, through the kindness of God, been etched into the very minds of men for their imitation.

The original on which our actions must be modelled is the unvarying story of God's dealings with men. He is our Father; by His omnipotent adoption, we are His sons, like Him not only in the life we lead but in the actions that proceed from that life. We reflect that divine treatment of men by a filial imitation of our Father in our treatment of men precisely as other sons of our Father, brothers in the Spirit by which we are all made sons of God. The identifying marks of our Father's treatment of men are justice and mercy; it will be these that must single out our days with men as distinct from any lesser social living.

God's justice is wise, deep, slow; unhurried by anger or incertitude, unmoved by superficialities, indifferent to its own justification in its regard for the happiness of men. It is a calm thing, perhaps more terrible for its very calmness which puts its fairness beyond question; a sure thing that denies no man his rights, and permissively bows to the surrender of those rights only when stubbornly insistent impenitence demands catastrophe. Too often we think of our Father's justice only in terms of judgment, and penalties that can neither be evaded nor appealed; this is a child's unkindness, taking the fatherly activity for granted unseeingly while it rages bitterly against correction. By far the most of God's just activity is positive, supplying the necessities for life, the means for growth, the helps for happiness; nowhere is that paternal justice more clearly seen than in His providence, His foresight, His unhurried patience, His steady thoughtfulness.

The divine mercy is not in conflict with God's justice. Rather, it goes far beyond the demands of justice, and far behind justice's beginnings. There is no place for justice until divine mercy has filled up the total deficiency of nothingness to bring men into being. From that first moment of life until its last, there will be in every man's life a steady flow from the divine superabundance to fill up the misery of human defects; a steady flow, unfailing and effective until the time when we insist upon divorcing mercy from justice and dam up our souls against the life-giving waters of divine benignity.

After that family model, our actions are oustandingly just. Justice becomes a consuming thirst within us, a thirst that is yet joyful in the achievement by others of what is their due. It will tolerate no compromise, have no truck with what happens to be legal but is odoriferously unjust, no toying with inducements to disregard others. Injustice in any of its forms is a stink in our nostrils, nauseating, revolting; its beckoning touch is not an allure but a befoulment from which we instantly recoil. So the full strength of meekness is exercised again and again to keep a firm hand on the reins of anger's violence lest it trample on men's rights or stand in the way of justice. Our mercy is alert, quick to see another's misery as keenly as though it were our own, and as quickly to minister to it. None of this is condemnatory of men, none of it proceeds from a condescending pity; for this is entirely a family affair, done by sons to their brothers. The sins, the weaknesses, the waverings of men are so like our own; their goals are so surely ours and our Father's.

Within this divine family which is now ours, we have the perfect model of divine social life in the incarnate natural Son of God; the pattern of our living is spelled out for our feeble eyes and minds as He becomes one of us and moves amongst us. He is our brother, by nature a son as we are by grace sons of the same Father. United to Him by this close family bond, we can understand and imitate the son who did all things whatsoever the Father commanded, the neighbor who showed mercy, the judge who turned aside vengeance when sorrow had already satisfied justice, the friend who gave His life for His friends. Our imitation of Him will be saturated with mercy, fragrant with gratitude, unyielding in veracity's adherence to truth; because He showed us how and is so ready to help us, we too can be strongly meek, truthfully humble, and open-handedly liberal. He is not only our brother but also our Savior, and thus the priestly father of all the supernatural sons of God generated by the power of His blood. The test of our love for Him is as sharp and concrete as the Ten Commandments; but the joy of it is not to be measured within any limits. He is ours. We walk down the same road; there is a family resemblance in our very gait; and a comfort not to be tasted by any but the family in that arm-in-arm companionship of the long way home.

Within the limits of our own purely human ranks, we have the perfect model of divine social living in Mary of Nazareth, the Mother of God. She, too, is an adopted child, needing all those same gifts of omnipotence to be at home in the family of God; yet so perfect were those gifts in her that God could make His home in her family. The difference between Mary's gifts and ours is not one of kind but of degree; she is one of ours, but blessed beyond all angels and saints with the divine gifts necessary to and flowing from her divine maternity. Her social virtues roll from our lips to make a complete litany of divinely human perfection: the humility of the Annunciation, the gratitude of the Magnificat, the modesty of the Nativity, the affability that gave so ready a welcome to Joseph, Elizabeth, shepherds, Magi, Simeon and Anna. The list defies completion. The relevant point here is that her life with men was a perfectly divinized social life for all its quiet, its obscurity, its poverty; unobtrusive to its very end, it yet flowed through the public life of her Son, shared the redemption of men in Calvary's death and gave of its nourishment to the infant Church. The sparse details of her living with men are jewels to be fondled tirelessly: her love of Joseph; her courage on the roads to Bethlehem, Egypt, Calvary and back to an empty Jerusalem; her graciousness to Elizabeth and the first pilgrims to the Cave; her surrender of her precious Infant to the aged arms of Simeon; her thoughtfulness at Cana; her loyalty at Calvary. When the whole pattern of her living among men is assembled, scarce though the details be, we see how perfectly she shows us if, without irreverence, we try to think of her in connection with any of the social vices: injustice, rudeness, lying, stinginess, meanness, savagery, brutality. The very thought wakes a horror in us; and we are right. It is not thus that we are to live with men; and the Mother of Jesus so lived among men as to be loved by the men of all the centuries.

Of course she is the Mother of men, for her Son is the brother of the adopted sons of God. Hers is a family interest in each one of us, for she is divinely mother, humanly sister; she is the one human person most perfectly at home in that divine family, most perfectly reflecting, then, the perfections of the Father in her life, an eternal life, among men. Of course she is the Mother of mercy, for the misery of each of us is seen as her own misery, a family affair for which something, everything must be done alertly, understandingly, lovingly. She is the handmaid of the Lord, giving Him from the beginning a child's wholehearted, unquestioning, utterly loyal service; proudly, eagerly, gratefully, humbly.

These models are steadily before the eyes of every practising Catholic. All the days are measured and judged by these patterns: Father, Son and Savior, and Holy Mother of God. Against the dismay of the fainthearted at such heights, by way of remedy for too much straining for the stars, there is another model close to our hearts and close indeed to our humble lives. We have said above that the Gift of Piety is concerned not with hard things but only with common, ordinary ones: or, more profoundly, that the Gift of Piety reduces all it touches to the common, the domestic level, the level of affairs of the family. The champion of common things is that just man, Joseph, the carpenter of Nazareth, head of the Holy Family and Protector of the Universal Church.

The stamp of the ordinary is deep in him, making him easily recognizable as just like ourselves. Here is a man who never finished the fight against poverty, a man handy with his hands whose day's work was the frail barrier of safety for his family; here is a man working among men, making his own way without patronage or advantage—indeed even his divine foster son worked no miracles in his favor. Yet, as is the way of little men, he measured up to the heroic on demand: against crowds and kings, lonely roads and foreign lands, cherishing the young husband's exquisite privilege of anxiety for his family. The briefest sketch of his living among men brings out sharply the strong man's gentleness, quiet courage, unquestioning trust of Mary, his complete loyalty, and unlimited generosity with his life, his strength, his labors. He was content with a place in the shadows if only his family were safe and happy. He did the ordinary things with such quiet perfection and, as is the way of so many fathers, was through all his days so unthinking of himself.

This is how we deal with men under the impulse of the Holy Spirit. This is not only what we do, but also how we do it: with all the ease, the grace, the smooth consistency of divine action, for this is social life divinely lived. We are the adopted sons of God; all our dealings are with the children of that same heavenly Father; our social life is an affair of the divine family. This is the proper mode of action in all our dealings with men. We can see it again and again in actions of practising Catholics with others: in family life, in neighborly ministrations, in the routine of the parish, the responsibilities of the community and nation, in business practices, in the fun and games that make up our recreation. Perhaps it comes more sharply to the fore in action for others: in the works of mercy which overflow from such family life as is ours, in our defense of others even against themselves, in all apostolic action. The perfection of social life through the Gift of Piety is an absolute requisite for all these activities. It will be perfectly clear, then, that those who by their very profession serve others have a special claim on omnipotence to this social perfection: priests, nuns, doctors, nurses, lawyers, teachers, tradesmen, and so on, live their professional lives under the impulse of this divine perfection or defeat the very purposes of their professions and become threats rather than servants to the men and women among whom they move.

The further significance of the completion of our adoption into the family of God through the Gift of Piety can perhaps be made more clear by a contrast that in our times is by no means theoretical. In a materialistic world, a man looks about him to see a world that is nobody's, that came from nowhere. The world is nobody's house; he himself has no family ties beyond those forged by biological accidents. He is obsessed by an animal ignorance of his own origin and the origin of the world. He must see himself and all other men as waifs adrift in chaos: here there is no omnipotent protection, no eternally wise foresight, no fatherly benignity. Nothing in the world lays claim to his respect, for nothing has any inherent excellence; there is no room for appreciation where there is no measure of worth; there is no point in respect, conservation, or prolonged effort where nothing is going to any particular goal. Men are street urchins fighting over a coin, refugees snatching at a loaf of bread, displaced persons in a world where mercy is a stranger. Each man is alone in the world, and all others are intruders on his life; individuals to be watched, fought, subdued, used. Contempt for the inanimate world that cannot strike back at him, and envy and hatred for men who are either his rivals or his slaves—these are the logical (and increasingly the factual) fruits of his living. To put it all in one word: here is homelessness, full blown, complete, devastating.

Under the guidance of the gift of Knowledge, Piety sends a man into a world that is the property of a Father whose sons we are. This is family property, fashioned, conserved, treasured with paternal wisdom. Every detail of that family property, then, deserves and gets respect, appreciation, and above all a penetration that eagerly recognizes each facet of divine perfection mirrored there. The inanimate world is a constant unveiling of the beauty, the goodness, the strength and the gentleness of our benign Father, and so still further proof of His benignity. The Gift of Piety busies us about the common things of home and all that belongs to the family. It replaces the homelessness of men, fulfilling men's perennial dream of home by extending the family life of heaven to the most secret recesses of the world.

It is a truth, readily established, that only children have homes. As they mature, they grow out of the homes in which they were born and set out to found their own homes; but the homes they found are homes for their children, not homes for themselves. At whatever age their own parents die, these present heads of families will have all the sense of loss, of exposure to hostility, of aloneness, of having home slip from their fingers. As parents, a man and woman are not at home; rather, they take on themselves God's role of protection, nourishment, foresight and all the other qualities of paternity. It is the children who are embraced and secured by these very paternal qualities. We have a home only as long as we are children; through the perfection of the Gift of Piety we do indeed become little children, our eyes are open to the fatherly benignity of God, the world is a part of our home, and we move with all the confidence of children in the wisdom, the strength, the love, and the care of our Father. It is hard for the stubborn pride of men to be at home, though their hearts give them no peace until that homecoming is accomplished; it is hard, for it demands the humility of children, a constant rebirth, a trust, a loyalty, a subordination that does not come easy to one engaged in playing the role of God to his own children. The Gift of Piety is the homemaker, preserving our tender youth by putting us completely at our ease in an eternal family. We can test our at-homeness, and so our status as children, by submitting our actions to the measure of sonship under our heavenly Father: the sons of this Father are those who show mercy, who keep His commandments, who give their life for His other sons, our friends.

The evidence of defect of this Gift of Piety is too easy to find in a world that gags at justice and lolls at ease in the filth of injustice. But there is no particular point in tracing the obvious; certainly there is nothing of comfort or inspiration in the self-inflicted tragedies of men who are homeless by choice. What is not so obvious, and yet is clearly there to be seen, is the evidence of this Gift of Piety at work in common people, at common things, divine sparks flashing at every human contact with men or with the world. There is a divine way to live with others: with God, with men, and with the world. God Himself has shown it clearly in the works of nature and supernature. It has been lived in detail and with divine perfection by the Son of God made man. For its utter human perfection, there is the perfect life of the Mother of God; lest we be abashed by such models, there is the quietly obscure Joseph to make the lesson plain to the most hesitant. This divinization of our social life, this at-homeness in the family of God, is the Holy Spirit's gift of Piety; a gift not given to be idle; a gift proper to everyone in the state of grace; and a gift that does in fact work on every level of Christian life.

Piety
(Summary from the Summa)

"... since it pertains properly to piety to repay obligations and reverence to one's father, it is a consequent that the piety by which, at the movement of the Holy Spirit, we pay worship and obligations to God as our Father, is a Gift of the Holy Spirit.

"To pay worship to God as Creator, as religion does, is more excellent than to pay reverence to one's own father in the flesh, as the piety which is a virtue does. To pay worship, however, to God as Father is even more excellent than to pay worship to God as Creator and Lord. Religion, therefore, is more important than the virtue of piety, but piety as the Gift is more important than religion.

"... by the Gift of Piety a man pays worship and obligations not only to God but also to all men on account of their relationship with God."

—Second of the Second Part, question one hundred twenty-one.

VII
The Poor and Their Fears
The Gift of Fear

The Poor and Their Fears

All men are in some sense poor and bound together, as is the way of the poor, by some kind of fear. This truth has walked the roads of the ages too long to be unrecognized. Ordinarily a single knock gains it ready admittance to the mind of any man; though youth may rush by it unheedingly, and a young age may be content to give it no more than a passing nod. If we could sit down with this truth for a quiet evening, tired and familiar as it is from its long travels, much could be learned. It might, for example, be asked: What makes men poor; what are men afraid of? Our smug serenity is not undisturbed when we hear that men are made poor by what they love, even when it enriches them, and much more so when it despoils them. Men are afraid to lose what they love, whether they cling to it in ecstasy or feel its entwining arms in horror.

For there is a foundation of human action which makes all men afraid in somewhat the same sense, or at least for the same kind of reason; and the first effect of that fear is poverty. Yet, in an apparent sameness of fear and poverty, there is a difference as wide as that between divinity and degradation. The one poor and fearful man has a heart scaling the heights of heaven even while his feet are dusty in the earth; another's mouth is bitter with the taste of hell's despair while health and strength still invigorate his bones.

It will be well worth while to tarry with this age-old truth at least long enough to learn why it is that all men are necessarily poor and fearful, and why each man is freely carried out of himself either by the secure fear of the blessed or the terror of the damned.

The learning of these lessons will not be simple. But, then, nothing human is simple. The lesser physical world moves along a path from which it cannot swerve, a path made simple by necessity; the angels wing their swift way untrammeled and undistracted. But men are a complex of these two worlds, dedicated by nature to complexity, to the clash, the echo, the interplay, and, at their best, the smooth harmony of flesh and spirit. It is not surprising, then, that poverty presents the same complexity as dims or brightens all our days; for man can and does meet poverty both in the material world and in the world of the spirit.

Material poverty too often elbows its way into the life of a man in complete disregard of his desires. To some men this unwelcome poverty strikes life as a blight, making a desert of it; the hot sun of desire, so fruitful in other lives, only serves to heighten the desolation of this man's life until he is eaten by fevered bitterness and revengeful frustration. Ultimately his bitterness demands more than poverty has denied him; it will be unsatisfied until other more fortunate men have been made to taste the dregs that have been his daily drink. Other men will bear this same material poverty as a burden rather than shrivel under it as a blight. To them, while it is unwelcome, poverty is not the ultimate tragedy which makes life unbearable. These are the reluctant but cheerful poor who find little that is charming in poverty, but who can live peacefully with it through a long lifetime because of ultimate horizons which shrink the purely material to the level of the secondary, if not the level of the insignificant. If a man forgets, or is robbed of, the knowledge that he is spirit as well as body, poverty destroys him; but if the splendid goals of the spirit are still his to reach for and possess, then poverty is as helpless as any other material thing to batter a man into the dirt.

Indeed, it has been possible for a few, because of the grace of God and the help of many other less fortunate but richer men, to search out poverty and welcome it into their lives with an eager embrace. These can choose poverty, and other men can understand their choice, because man is soul as well as body, because material possessions can be seen as hindrances to a much more pressing activity and a much more desirable way of life.

Material poverty, then, is relatively simple in the complex human world. It is a bitter desolation, an annoying burden, or an exultantly chosen release. But at least it is not a subtle or hidden thing apt to trip up our stumbling minds in odd places. It is always found in those we can readily, visibly, tangibly locate as the poor. Poverty of spirit is something else again. If we define it broadly as the release of the soul from the enticement of all things other than the concrete supreme objective of this individual's life, poverty of spirit will range from a spiritual pauperism of degradation to the spiritual wealth of the Beatitudes. Poverty of spirit in this sense has no necessary connection with material wealth or with material poverty. It is not only true that it can be found among the rich as well as among the poor; it is demonstrably certain that absolutely no man or woman escapes it; we are all, without exception, poor with a poverty of spirit, whether it be a poverty that debases us or a poverty that ennobles us.

A glance around any large city, or a spark of imagination for that matter, furnishes sufficient evidence of the fears that beset the materially reluctant poor. There are fears of unemployment, of sickness, of old age, of the care of the children, and a hundred others. Not that these are the exclusive terrors of the materially poor; they are, in one way or another, also the fears of the rich, but they are an immediate, and often terrifying, threat to the poor. Our concern for the moment is not with these fears which make such completely justified demands on the justice and charity of men. Surely these fears merit concern; but our intellectual powers of mastication and digestion restrict us to small bites of truth, however great our hunger. It will be all that we can handle to concentrate on the fears that give rise to poverty of spirit.

Poverty of spirit presupposes a hierarchy of goals, a scale of values at whose peak is the supreme objective of this individual man. Obviously, when we speak in terms of a supreme objective, the inference is that there are lesser objectives which fit under that last and unchallenged one. It is precisely the relegation of these lesser objectives to their proper, and so secondary, place that constitutes poverty of spirit as we have defined it. Not that this is an arbitrary arrangement, or a special set of conditions which men must be argued into constructing or which they can hope, somehow, to escape. Whether he likes it or not, every human being must have a supreme objective, a last goal, before he can produce a single action, even so simple an action as taking a step or speaking a word. For action is a movement to a goal; and it is just as impossible for this rational creature, man, to take a step to nowhere as it is for him to take the same step in several directions at the same time. He may change his supreme objective from hour to hour or day to day, or he may retain it as supreme for the whole length of life and eternity; but supreme goal he must have, or he stands in frozen immobility.

In the supernatural order, that supreme objective will be God, placed at the top of this man's scale of values by his love of God above all things, by the infused virtue of charity. It could, of course, be said here that God is also at the top of the scale of values in the natural order; but it would be much more to the point to usher the hypothetical natural order out of the room at once. In this way we can avoid the confusion which might easily arise from having a discussion interrupted by ghostly whispers from nonexistent things. The fact is that man never has and never will work out his life in a natural order. He was created in grace, lifted to a supernatural life from the first instant, and privileged to work out his destiny in a supernatural state ever since. The natural is not destroyed but rather perfected by grace; the point here is that it simply does not exist alone. For each man, it is either heaven or hell, God or the devil;

there is no refuge for the timid in a colorless, neutral state of nature. When reference is made here to an order other than the supernatural order, we are dealing with factual orders, ignoring the hypothetical with its speculative allurements; the pressure of the facts is urgent.

In any order, then, less than the supernatural (which means in all orders opposed to the supernatural goal of God), there will be a parallel supreme objective, a substitute for God. This substitute will often be horrible, but is nonetheless a real parallel. If God is not this man's supreme objective here and now in this action, then something else is. In either case the supremacy of this particular objective necessitates the discarding of all other really or apparently desirable things as supreme, to be held to at all costs. The facts of the matter are that, in any crucial action, a rival making claim to the throne of our hearts must go down to defeat before the supremacy of this one object which is the source of all our action. The supreme objective, or last goal, of this man at this time sets up his subjective norm of what is desirable and what is hateful, however much this norm may conflict with the truth of things, and however much the individual himself may perversely see this conflict with truth and ignore it.

To say that we have chosen one ultimate objective of our life and action is to say that we are in love with that which seems to us so eminently desirable, in love with it to the point of dedication to it. From that love, that dedication, whether the love be noble or ignoble, there follows, as an effect from a cause, a great fear: the fear of the loss of the loved object, the fear of separation from it, the fear of having this other self of ours cut off from us.

In the supernatural order, this fear is a gift of the Holy Ghost which goes by the name of Fear of the Lord; a habit infused into the soul by God along with sanctifying grace and the theological and the moral virtues. It is the first of the Gifts of the Holy Ghost in the order of ascent, the last in the order of descent, for it lays the foundation for the work of all the other gifts. All these Gifts of the Holy Ghost make our souls readily, easily responsive to the movement of the Holy Ghost. The Gift of Fear removes the fundamental impediment to such responsiveness by doing away with any rebellion, indeed with even the trace of repugnance, in our subjection to the divine Mover. For by the Fear of the Lord we fly from the awful evil of separation or loss of our supremely loved One by our eager subjection to Him and the more and more penetrating reverence for all that is His.

In common with the other Gifts of the Holy Ghost, Fear of the Lord operates, not in the human manner, but in the angelic, or rather in the divine, manner. That is, it moves into action, not as a result of an argued conviction which can be retraced from conclusion to principles, but rather its action is an instantaneous thing, swifter than instinct's response; nor is it to be understood by retracing steps by which it came about, for there are no steps. Its action will remain inexplicably mysterious and luminously intelligent, for it is in the divine mode. Thus, for example, a temptation to mortal sin (which is a temptation to supplant God by a rival) can be rejected in one of two ways: by an argued conviction that, while this rival has its good points and is undoubtedly appealing to some of our appetites, we can have it only at the cost of rejecting God; or by striking out against the temptation with an instantaneous aversion. In the first case, we conquer the temptation with, perhaps, a touch of reluctance remaining in our appetites; in the second, it is as though, sickened by the repulsiveness of loss of God, we vomit out the poisonous thought.

Because we are so completely on God's side by Fear of the Lord, through our reverence for and subjection to Him, Charity can unite us more and more intimately with the God we love so. Rivals to, even distractions from, this union are so utterly routed by this Gift of the Holy Ghost that love's uniting action goes on its swift way unimpeded. As a result we find it necessary to get something of that air of union into our very name for the fear. We call it "filial fear," hinting at sonship and the close union between a loving father and a loved son; or "chaste fear," making reference to the intimacy of marital union, the dissolution of which is a kind of dismemberment. Both are clumsy, inadequate terms that give only a vague notion of a union surpassing, in its very first instant, any other union in this world. Effected directly by Charity and indirectly by Fear of the Lord, this union increases step by step with the increase of Charity. As Charity grows, so does this reverential subjection which is Fear of the Lord, for we are the more intolerant of rivals or of separation from the infinite Good as we love Him more.

In a less than supernatural order, that is, where a substitute for God is at the top of our scale of desirable things, it will still hold true that the immediate effect of this love for God's substitute generates a fear of its loss or of separation from it.[1] Man fears to lose what he loves, however debasing his love may be. The substitutes for God may be, or approach, the immaterial: such things as one's own self, honor, glory, or power. Or they may be grossly material and obviously beneath the dignity of human nature: such things as riches, carnal pleasure, food, or drink. Whatever the substitute chosen by this man at this time, the fear to which it gives birth will beat off all rivals, beginning with God Himself, by the very thoroughness of the subjection and horrible reverence which it pours into a

[1] No mention has been made of cowardice, the vice opposed to fortitude; nor has there been any account here of the passion of fear. This mundane fear, the fear in question throughout, is obviously a form of moral cowardice, a flight from things that should not be run from; and the extreme form of it. The lesser forms are not here pertinent. In the interest of completeness, there should be some detailed treatment of the six varieties of the passion of fear which St. Thomas distinguishes, since this mundane fear does deteriorate, with the blinding of the intellect through adherence to worldly things, to more and more of an animal fear and, in the later stages, is easily recognized as overwhelmingly an animal drive.

man's heart. This substitute is supreme for this man; it is to be given the complete subjection due the ultimate goal; and all else must be sacrificed that this be maintained. For him, this is the supremely desirable thing.

The work of this fear will vary according to the particular substitute for God which has turned this man's life upside down. Whatever its particular objects, this fear will, in its manner of operation, maintain a horrifying resemblance to the Fear of the Lord. It is mundane, not supernatural; but it will, as it increases, have more and more of the instinctive, unthinking rapidity of absolute aversion from the rivals which lay siege to a man's heart. In the case of the Gift of Fear, the angelic mode of action is from the elevation of man's mind and heart to higher levels, from a luminosity of intellect that is more than human, from the sway of *intelligence* superseding *rationality*. It makes men see more deeply, more quickly, more truly. The mundane fear achieves swift counteroffensives, not by perfecting man's mind but by blinding it. The action is more and more instinctive in the sense of more and more animal until, eventually, even the human level seems a dizzily high and foreign peak. Given time, the glutton cannot lift his eyes off his plate, the proud man cannot pull himself away from his mirror.

We become what we love. The lover is in the loved one, and the loved one is in the lover; love and union are correlative terms. These truths point to one of the most disgusting of the implications of this substitution for God and its consequent mundane fear. For this mundane fear is also, in some sense, "filial" and "chaste"; in the repulsive sense, that is, of making a man so closely one with lust, gluttony, avarice (or whatever the particular substitute) as to simulate the union of father and son, the intimacy of the union of husband and wife.

As this union of vice increases, so does the fear of the loss of this vice. As the fear grows steadily greater, it reaches, in the case of immaterial substitutes for God, a degree of mania in a miasma of distrust and suspicion. In the case of the material substitutes, particularly in the case of carnal pleasure, the very fear of loss of these pleasures nourishes a kind of horror of *not* losing them, and is gradually consumed by this horror to melt into despair, forging the last link in the chains of slavish subjection to unspeakable degradation.

It might be argued here that this discussion has failed to distinguish between man's rational and his animal or sense loves. Thus it might be conceded that, while man can substitute for God things that can be loved rationally (man himself, honor, glory, power—the immaterial things), from the very nature of sense love, the material objects cannot be substitutes for God. They are used, as the animals use them, to the destruction of the loved objects and the utility of the animal or the man. As a matter of fact, however, only in the insane and in infants is there found a purely animal love in men. In all other instances, even the things that are the primary objects of the sense appetites are loved rationally. As St. Thomas says, it is ridiculous to speak of friendship with a horse or with wine, since there can be no mutual return of love, nor can there be any altruism in such love. Nevertheless, what man loves to the destruction of the loved object (as do the animals) can, because man is man, be loved to man's own destruction. His rational nature allows indefinite horizons to his physical appetites which, so indulged, become masters to enslave a man—a thing impossible in the animals. Man can and does subject himself to the things beneath him. He does make a god out of the things meant to serve him. And he gives this god the worship of sacrifice of all else to it.

In the supernatural order the first act of the Fear of the Lord will be the beatitude of Poverty of Spirit. For the first act of this Gift of the Holy Ghost is an act of complete subjection to God and utmost reverence for Him, or, from the other side of the picture, flight from what threatens our union with God. A man perfectly subject to God, a man moved by Fear of the Lord, does not seek greatness or fulfillment outside of God, either in himself or in external things such as honor, glory, riches, or power; such self-inflation is directly opposed to Fear of the Lord, so the avoidance of such inflation is a direct consequence of that Fear and is Poverty of Spirit. In more concrete terms, the man whose goal is God is humble against the dangers of pride by reason of his fear of loss of God; he is liberal and generous, counting lightly all things less than God; he easily reaches magnificence in his works and plans, for great things are by no means overwhelming to one in the embrace of God; and so, almost as a matter of course, he is magnanimous, great-souled, in his concentration on the few things of momentous concern, and his release from the complexity of numberless trifles.

Pleasure is not nearly so difficult a thing to keep off the throne of our hearts as is personal greatness; pleasure's threats lie rather in its allure, its soft, enervating enticements. The man who is perfectly subject to God, revering Him, loving Him above all else, finds his principal joy in God, not in things less than God. So the fruits of the Holy Ghost which pertain to the moderate use of or abstinence from temporal things, such fruits as modesty, continence, chastity, are fruits of the Fear of the Lord. As a man cannot be perfectly subject to God and puffed up in himself with pride, so neither can he revere God without that reverence being extended to the image of God which is man.

It is of some importance to see the whole picture of man as he is perfected by the Gift of Fear. It is not too hard to grasp something of the perfection and attractiveness of the solidly humble man who is generous, liberal, great in soul, magnificent in his works. But it is easy to miss the profound significance of the consequences of this Gift of Fear in the order of temperance. Modesty, continence, and chastity are all lesser parts of the cardinal virtue of temperance and communicate in its common work of releasing the breathtaking splendor of the individual soul to let it shine forth through the infinite details of a man's personal life. Thus modesty, one of the echoes of man's reverence for God, is that reverence for man which is concentrated on individual human beauty; it insists on the human and individual luster of the soul shining forth in such details as one's dress, work, play, study of truth. By its very nature as a revelation of beauty, it is the sworn enemy of ugliness, of every irreverence to the human individual that would make anything about him other than the splendidly human thing it is. Continence is the seasoned fighter that guards the inviolable sanctuary of a man's soul against the rush of passion. Continence, then, is that same reverence for man concentrating on the high dignity of man, insisting on human control in the material where distortion and ugliness are most easily introduced, the field of his sense appetites. While chastity is that same reverence insisting on the splendor of human beauty as against the frenzy of animals by focusing on the absolute consecration which is an integral part of the language of love, above all in its highest physical expression.

It is clear, then, that the Poverty of Spirit which corresponds to the Holy Ghost's Gift of Fear is quite the opposite of spiritual pauperism. It does mean that a man is spiritually stripped of the impediments to untrammeled love and union with God; that he is poor in passing trifles that he may be rich in eternally enduring, infinite Good. The emphasis, in spite of the term "poverty," is much more on keeping our arms full than in emptying them of things that will ultimately paralyze those arms. As the fear born of love of God is not a dark terror but rather the tight grasp of a child's eager hand or the lover's reverent multiplication of his life in "another self," so the poverty which is the first effect of that fear is not a despoiling of a man's soul, a kind of bitter spiritual beggary, but an enriching of the soul beyond the wildest dreams of men.

This man, who is penetrated by the Fear of the Lord with its consequent Poverty of Spirit, appears before his fellows in any age as all that a man should be and much more: humble, generous, liberal, magnificent, magnanimous; reverent of human beauty in its smallest details of daily life, reverent of human dignity, consecrated to the victorious surrender of love.

In any order less than the supernatural, where a substitute has been found for God on the throne of our heart, it is equally true that the reverence and subjection we give this usurper has its echoes and consequences all down through the life of man. Obviously this man is easily proud, for by his choice of a substitute for God he has striven for a personal aggrandizement in preference to divine service; at least he is a victim of a pride which forbids him to bend the knee in adoration seeking forgiveness, and for as long as the substitution endures. In place of generosity and liberality, he is committed to a penny-pinching stinginess, because this substitute he has chosen cannot be shared without being lost; even time wears it down, and any breath of frank honesty may topple it from its throne. He does not dare expose it openly in the marketplace, let alone invite others to make themselves at home with it. He is inevitably petty, small-souled, since this substitute he has chosen is a small, limited, circumscribed thing; for the most part, it is much smaller than the soul of man himself, and by the very fact of embracing it a man dedicates himself to a steady shrinking, shriveling of soul. He becomes narrower, tighter, meaner, more despicable as this perverse love more fully conquers all of his being.

It is absurd to look to this man for reverence of human things, since his fundamental choice, the primary direction of his life, is itself a betrayal of his own human nature. It is not surprising that he brushes to one side the considerations of human beauty; perhaps by taking the splendor of the spirit out of it, to parade it as a purely physical, animal thing; and ultimately to distort even the physical to the point of obvious ugliness. This will seep down through all the details of a man's life: his work, his play, his clothes, his search for truth. In place of reverent concern for man's dignity, he will be a snickering champion of degradation; rather than reverent consecration, he will find baseness an increasingly familiar and easy way of life.

This mundane fear, which is born of a substitution of a rival for God, has its own immediate consequent of poverty of spirit in the rejection of all that threatens the continued supremacy of the substitute; and here the poverty is absolute destitution, complete pauperism. Its final result is a complete rout of the pretensions put forth to entice men from God: a man who is proud, stingy, petty, committed to ugliness, degradation, baseness. Even in a pagan age, such a one, when he has come to the full fruition of his fear and poverty, is a pariah among men.

The picture seems overdrawn, particularly when specific instances come immediately to mind of proud men who are not base, libertines who are generous, misers who are not proud, and so on. Actually this is not a refutation but a confirmation of the basic contrast between the Fear of the Lord, with its Poverty of Spirit, and the mundane fear and spiritual pauperism which are their parallels. All the consequences of filial fear of God always follow, whereas the parallel "filial fear" of God's substitute does not have all its consequences in any one subject. It might well be that a man is base without pride or stinginess; the proud may be without ugliness in some details, though not in all. But the humble are also, and always, generous, liberal, magnanimous, modest, continent, chaste. There is, you see, no unity in evil; some evils are incompatible with others; nor is it necessary to have all vices in order to be vicious. On the other hand, all the virtues are necessarily connected: it is not enough to have one virtue to be virtuous; indeed, it is impossible to have only one virtue; if any are to be had, all must be had.

Deeper reasons for this chaotic and fragmentary character of evil in contrast to the order and integrity of good can be had either from the side of man or from the side of the hierarchy of good which spurs him on to action. From the side of man, no man can be utterly evil, he cannot be totally corrupted, so always there must be something of evil lacking in the most vicious of men. Total corruption would mean annihilation: an impossible thing. Evil is a canker, eating away at the only thing that supports it: for if you are to have a bad spot in an apple, something of the apple must be left to harbor that corruption; if you are to have a hole in a fence, something of the fence must be left, or even the hole disappears; if you are to have vice in man, something of human goodness must still be left to furnish a home for the viciousness. From the side of the hierarchy of goods which a man sets up by his choice of a final goal, it is clear that if he chooses to consider the lowest step as the top of the stairs, the rest must come tumbling down in useless chaos, or he is refuted by the facts. When man pushes God out of his heart and enthrones a substitute, he throws out the highest and last of the steps his heart should take and selects a substitute somewhere down the line, usually toward the very bottom. All the rest is torn down to clutter up his life with confusion added to fundamental chaos.

From this contrast of the Fear of the Lord with mundane fear, of Poverty of Spirit with spiritual pauperism, some interesting conclusions stand out. It must be admitted, at the very outset, that fear is inescapable by any man and is therefore absolutely universal, because man cannot live without love of some final goal; this love decrees that man fear the loss of what is loved. Such fear, universal to all men, will be either the genuine filial fear which is the Gift of the Holy Ghost, or a ghastly counterfeit which is a deadly parallel. In either case, that fear will underline the intimate unity which our love has created; underline, in other words, the fact that we are one with this loved object as a child is one with his parents, or a husband one with his wife, these comparisons being the best of many clumsy expressions of a unity that is ineffable or unspeakable. In either case, that fear will universally have inescapable consequences: ennobling in the case of filial fear, inevitably degrading and corrupting in the case of its counterfeit. It will have been noted that the very things which stand out as proclaimed objectives in the development of man in our time can be had only by subjection to and reverence for God: generosity, magnificence, magnanimity, beauty, dignity. But they must be taken along with humility and consecration. On the other hand, the things which are most earnestly detested are the inevitable consequences of the counterfeit of filial fear: stinginess, pettiness, ugliness, degradation. It has proved possible to enshrine baseness and pride; it has not yet proved feasible to enshrine stinginess and pusillanimity in the public mind, though ugliness is well on its way to full toleration. Probably the day will never come when the full consequences of counterfeit fear will be embraced by men, for, after all, man is not susceptible of total corruption. It is only by the embrace of all the effects of genuine filial fear that the heart of man can hope for happiness: for even the human dreams of men find their fulfillment only in the divine.

Fear

(*Summary from the* Summa)

"... three fears are concerned with punishment, but in different ways. Worldly, or human, fear is concerned with punishment that turns men away from God, which the enemies of God at times inflict or threaten; servile and initial fear, on the other hand, are concerned with a punishment by which men are drawn to God, and which is inflicted or threatened by God. Servile fear is concerned with this punishment principally, whereas initial fear is concerned with it secondarily. ... Initial fear stands in the same relationship to filial fear as imperfect to perfect Charity. ... We must conclude, therefore, that initial fear ... does not differ essentially from filial fear. ...

"... the fear of God which is numbered among the seven Gifts of the Holy Spirit is filial, or chaste, fear ... the Gifts of the Holy Spirit are habitual perfections of the powers of the soul, by which these are made amenable to the movement of the Holy Spirit, just as by the moral virtues the appetitive powers are made amenable to the motion of reason. ... For a thing to be amenable to the motion of any mover, the first necessary condition is that it should be not a resistant subject of the mover, since resistance of the movable subject to the mover hinders the movement. This is what filial, or chaste, fear does, because by it we revere God and avoid separating ourselves from Him. ... Filial fear necessarily increases when Charity grows, just as an effect increases with the increase of its cause. ... Filial fear does not imply a separation from God but a submission to Him, and it avoids separation from that submission."

—Second of the Second Part, question nineteen, passim.

VIII
Tranquil Violence
The Gift of Fortitude

Tranquil Violence

"Fear not, Mary." The angelic words were more than a comfort, they were an authentication. Mary must have heard them with something of the blessed sense of repose and solace that comes from old, familiar, cherished things; relaxing, as we do in a physical tribute to familiar streets, well-loved rooms, intimate friends. For these were indeed familiar words. They had rung out from the sacred writings with all the frequency and music of a soft-tongued bell of later ages. They would be inevitable in Isaias, seeing the Messiah through the veil of prophecy: "Fear ye not the reproach of men, and be not afraid of their blasphemies." "Fear not, for I am with you." They would be echoed again and again in the songs of David, particularly in those that looked to the Savior: "I will not fear thousands"; "For though I should walk in the midst of the shadow of death, I will fear no evils, for Thou art with me"; "The Lord is my light and salvation, whom shall I fear, . . . of whom shall I be afraid, . . . my heart shall not fear"; "Therefore we shall not fear when the earth shall be troubled, . . . the God of Jacob is our protector"; "I will not fear what flesh can do against me."

The blessed words were to become still more familiar, still more dear to Mary and to all the world to whom she gave her Son; for they were to become peculiarly His, a beloved reiteration of His divine solicitude. "Fear not, only believe"; "Have a good heart, it is I, fear ye not"; "Fear not, little flock"; "Let not your heart be troubled, nor let it be afraid"; "Be of good heart." Inevitably the strengthening words would be said again and again, for who of us can love and not reach out to rescue, to protect a loved one battered by waves of fear? Men have enough to fear, God knows. Knowing it to all the detailed depths of divine wisdom, He could not but be eager, even constrained, to quiet those fears in view of the limitless love He harbored for men. Here we are not dealing with fears that can be hidden from loved eyes, or love that can be blind, power that can be helpless; but with the all-seeing eye of God, the love that would go to and beyond the limits of the Eucharist and the Cross, the power that opens the most secret doors of a man's heart and enters as one to whom this territory is familiar.

The Gospel story gives us a hint of the frequency with which that "Fear not" fell from the divine lips of the Savior. The gloom of the Last Supper, where the apostles faced the fact of separation from the Master, tells us something of what that steady reassurance had meant to the hearts of men. The apostolic courage that conquered the world for Christ tells us beyond all doubt of the effectiveness of the assurance of God. Fear not, be of good heart, have courage. Why? Because you are weaklings, timid, cowardly, unable to stand on your own feet? Not at all. But because you have things to do that are much too much for the strength of men, heights to scale, choices to make, time and sorrow to batter down for eternity and joy; because, in a word, you are to walk in mystery on a divine level to a mysterious destiny that properly belongs to God.

There are indeed things to fear, attacks to face, burdens to be borne before which millions of men and women will cringe and flee. On our own poor human level, we come to the rescue of our friends by offering them the comfort of our presence, the resources of our strength, the willingness of our love. Pitiful as these things are, their effectiveness against fear is often astounding. Yet we cannot put heart into our friends; we can but summon the courage we know, or at least hope, is buried there; summon it and give it the little support that comes from our help, a help that is purely extrinsic, forever limited to the outer regions of a man's life. On this score, the sons of God have good reasons for summoning up their courage. The divine Friend offers the assistance of omnipotence, the reckless willingness of infinite love. Lest that intangible help slide out of our awareness, with our concern for tangible things, there is the living presence of the Son of God, walking among men, keeping His eternal vigil on the altar. For our purely human comfort, there is the bond that makes up our common life with all the saints living and dead, our family ties that make our fears a family concern and call to our assistance the gigantic resources of the ages which have looked to or sprung from the central power of the Cross.

Yet all this is still a matter of summoning up a courage that is already within a man's heart; sustaining, supporting it by bringing to his dangers and labors extra strength, the lives, the hearts, the minds, the hands of the millions of friends, even of a divine Friend, to whose loyalty he can lay claim. If the antidote for fear went no farther than that, it would be unworthy of the power and love of God; for that power and love can reach within the very soul of a man. We can, then, expect from our divine Friend not only the extrinsic help of His strength, but a positive infusion of courage within our very hearts. The "Fear not" of our Lord was much more than a word of solace; His "Be of good heart" was not a wish, an exhortation, but also a statement of a divinely accomplished fact: an announcement of the infusion into the soul of man of that Christian courage by which a man is less fearful, not only because of his friends, but because he is made brave.

That courage within a man's own soul is essential if he is to follow Christ. For our Lord's "Fear not" was not at all a divine coddling of the weakness of men; it must be heard in union with His prophecy, even His promise, of a terrifying violence. He told the apostles what they could expect from the world they were to conquer: persecution, exile, suffering, and death. They would meet violence as inevitably and as consistently as a man breasts wind driving down a road; what is more, they would travel with violence as a close companion, they would not only meet violence but bring it to bear on the world. They were not only to stand up under suffering, they were to be the violent ones before whom the powers of evil would flinch and flee. For it was His own clear statement that told them He had come to bring the sword into play, that the kingdom of heaven suffered violence, that it would be the violent who would bear it away. To take up a cross and follow Him would take courage: not only the courage to bear up under the cross, but the courage to bring that cross to men and women across the world, across the ages. His followers in every age would be the tranquilly violent men whose discomfort would be not only the result of the violence of enemies inflicted upon them, but the violence of a divine fire raging within them, and from them spreading to set the world afire. Here was another of those divine paradoxes that startled a world awake to the fact that God was made man and dwelt among men: Fear not; the kingdom of heaven suffereth violence. On both counts, courage was demanded; a courage greater than man can muster by years of brave living; a courage that would have to come within his soul from the Master who demanded so much from men and did so much more than He ever demanded.

There is in every man a double sense appetite to equip him to deal with the enticement of good things and the challenge or terror of hard things. Of course, there is a parallel activity in man's intellectual appetite, or will, on a scale as wide and far as the mind of man can see; when man is given the eyes of God through faith, the will of man reaches out to infinite good which properly belongs to God. Both the good things and the hard things can represent obstacles to the following of Christ, to the attainment of God; so man needs the virtuous perfection of his appetites to free him of these possibly disastrous impediments. We are not, for the moment, concerned with the difficulties encountered from the allure of good things. Our interest at the moment is with the difficult things and the perfection of our appetites in protection against whatever hindering effects the hard things can have on a man's swift return to God.

If man's life were neatly partitioned off into natural and supernatural sections, we would still be forced to relegate the naturally difficult things to an insignificant place in the scale of hard things a man must do and face. Actually, there is no such partition. We live in a supernatural order, destined for a supernatural end for which natural virtues are no direct help; at best these perfections against natural difficulties are no more than favorable dispositions removing impediments to the operation of the supernatural or infused virtues. Only these latter are equipment adequate for the actual end to which man's steps are directed; they alone measure up to the hard things, whether the difficulty has a natural look about it or not. The point is we must all take hurdles supernaturally if we are to finish the course and win the crown.

The divine extravagance with which this need of ours is met gives new depths to the constant "Fear not" of the fearless Christ. At the moment of baptism, when sanctifying grace floods our souls with divine life, the infused virtues which perfect the irascible appetite (the appetite that deals with hard things) come to us in all their divine perfection and extravagant variety. There is fortitude or courage, the martyr's virtue, to equip us for dangers and difficulties on the heroic scale, particularly the danger of death. Greatness of soul (magnanimity) keeps us safe from presumption, ambition, vanity, and pettiness. Magnificence puts our works on a level to match the greatness of soul, pushing stinginess out of our lives. By these two we are equipped to deal with the difficulty inherent in greatness. Against sorrow, which needs no greatness to make it difficult, there is patience. Perseverance protects us from both softness and stubbornness by enabling us to measure up to the difficulty inflicted on mortal man by the ceaseless blows of time.

Despite the divine magnificence in so equipping man to live divinely and for divine ends, still more is necessary. In a sense, the infused virtues given so graciously by God are too good for man; at least they are too big for him. He is a pygmy wielding the weapons of a giant; without further help, he is awkward, slow, fumbling, in a condition that would be disastrous, considering the difficulties he must meet and the angelic intelligences that are ranged against him. He needs still further divine help, a help that will enable him to move in a divine mode, not clumsily, slowly, and awkwardly, but swiftly, surely. He needs a Gift of the Holy Ghost; in this particular matter, the Gift of Fortitude or courage.

We easily push aside a serious consideration of the Gift of Fortitude as being a matter for academic discussion as far as the ordinary Catholic is concerned. These things are for the handful of saints in their physical or spiritual martyrdom; for the rest of us, we putter along doing the little things that make up the bulk of our routine days, having no more traffic with martyrdom than to give it our unstinting admiration. The high gifts of God are not for the average Catholic. Really, we should know better than this. Certainly one of the effects of the incarnation of the Son of God was to make such a mistake forever implausible. It should be almost enough that He stooped to take on our lowly nature for God's interest in lowly things to be abundantly clear. That He cast His life among the poor and spent His efforts preaching the gospel to them; that His divine power was exercised on the lepers, the outcasts, the sick, the dying, and the dead, beginning from the rescue of the humble hosts at Cana to the final crowning of the dying thief on Calvary; that His chosen disciples were poor fishermen and His greatest love was poured out on sinners: surely all this should make us hesitate to limit the generosity of God or His interest in the least of men. The Gift of Fortitude is a high gift of God indeed; but it is a gift given to everyone in the state of grace, a gift indispensable for salvation, and hence a gift that must be at work in the most routine day of the average Catholic. It is a common characteristic of the Gifts of the Holy Ghost that they are all in the soul of everyone in the state of grace.

The second common characteristic of all these gifts is their common effect of fluid mobility under the movement of the Holy Ghost. The giant weapons put in our pygmy hands are, by these gifts, put into smooth, swift action; so that, pygmies as we are, we produce gigantic works. The actions that flow from the virtues under the impetus of the Gifts of the Holy Ghost have little of the human about them beyond their immediate authors. It is we who produce these acts, but in a manner that forever leaves the world, and especially ourselves, mystified. For that manner is a divine manner by which our actions light up our days with the suddenness and glory of a tropic sunrise, their swift certainty defying analysis, since the step-by-step procedure that makes analysis possible is entirely absent from these divinely human acts.

The divine mode of the gifts has its only possible explanation in a participation, a sharing, of something divine. Thus, in explaining the way the Gift of Knowledge operates, St. Thomas says: "God's knowledge is not discursive or argumentative, but absolute and simple, to which that knowledge is likened which is a gift of the Holy Ghost, since it is a *participated likeness* thereof." Since the Gift of Fortitude deals primarily with the irascible or emergency appetite of man, it will face the heights and depths of hope and despair, the recklessness of daring, the terrors of fear, and the battering violence of anger. By the gift, then, something divine appears in the midst of the turbulence of man's dealing with hard things: deeper than serenity, stronger than tranquillity; something, indeed, of the assured confidence of God. By this gift we see man facing the turmoils and difficulties of his life with something like the stature of the divine Governor of the world looking out over the turmoils and wars wrought by the rebellious will of men attempting to overthrow His divine government.

The Gift of Fortitude does, indeed, primarily perfect the virtue of fortitude and thus is the ultimate preparation of the martyrs; but it would be a mistake to limit its divine lightning to the sustaining of dangers. Its field is almost as wide as the life of a man, for it reaches out to a winged conquest of all that is hard. In that whole field, the gift of fortitude steadily and divinely conquers fear and nourishes confidence. As a result a man's soul, under the influence of this gift, enjoys complete tranquillity in regard to the tempest of the irascible appetite, a serene confidence of completing all good works and avoiding all dangers, and thus inevitably an increasingly sharp desire for virtuous works.

Properly to appreciate this gift, it is of prime importance that we look at it in the light of the things we know so well. This matter of difficulty: how much of really hard things do we meet, things in which we stand in need of no less than God's own help? Lest we be embarrassed by admitting it, let the saints tell us that virtue is hard. Thus St. Augustine insists: "Those who desire to enjoy true goods, and wish to avoid loving earthly and material things, must toil." St. Thomas brings out the same truth more explicitly when he says that virtue is hard, while it is very hard to do virtuous deeds with an insatiable desire; that is, without the wavering into the bypaths that take us away from the goal of virtue, which is God. No one of us, with this encouragement, but can admit that it is not easy to keep the Ten Commandments. What else are we saying, in admitting the difficulty of virtue, than confessing that it is hard to follow Christ, hard to be perfect as our heavenly Father is perfect, hard to keep our eyes from being blinded to divine beauty by the glitter of the shatterings of divine beauty that lie all about us in creation?

The solid difficulty of virtue is accentuated by two familiar truths. It is no secret to us that every virtue tugs at any restraint put upon it in its eagerness to reach to its greatest heights; the honesty of an upright man is never satisfied by a justice that avoids prison, nor is purity content with merely avoiding obscenity. The virtues are good habits that can be perfected indefinitely; and they chafe at less than the best. Then, too, there is the extremely personal element in virtue's difficulty which makes it impossible to gather together a batch of objectively "hard virtues" and let the Gift of Fortitude do its work in their material. Each one of us, by reason of his individual temperament, finds some virtues easy to practice and some vices hard to avoid. Each of us, then, has his own corps of somewhat battered and battle-weary virtues that can never actually be withdrawn from the thick of the fight; we have, in other words, not only the universal difficulty of all virtue to face, we, each of us, have our own specially worrisome and intractable difficulties from which only death or God Himself can rescue us.

It is significant, in this matter of difficulty, that the theologians find the directive, or intellectual element, of fortitude in the Gift of Counsel which, they add, deals only with hard things. This Gift of Counsel, though it directly perfects the virtue of prudence, is directive of the Gift of Fortitude because of their common occupation with hard things. The implication is plain once we understand that prudence directed by the Gift of Counsel is busy getting things done; its work is the discovery of fitting means, a judgment of the best, and an effective application of this means to the attainment of the goal in sight. In other words, there is a steady difficulty for every one of us in such an apparently routine matter as making up our minds and moving into action. The difficulty is made explicit beyond all misunderstanding when St. Thomas explains: "Since, however, human reason is unable to grasp the singular and contingent things which may occur [and man's actions are always in the singular, contingent order], the result is that *the thoughts of mortal men are fearful, and our counsels uncertain* (Wisd. 9, 14). Hence, in search of counsel, man requires to be directed by God, who comprehends all things." Each of our acts has its own difficulties of uneasiness, uncertainty, and timidity. We do indeed need something of the courage of God.

From these considerations alone, the necessity of the Gift of Fortitude for every man is evident; because every man must practice virtue, every man has his own particularly difficult virtues, every man must, each day of his life, put forth decisive action. The necessity of the gift is thus plain; its beauty is best revealed in its less general field of the virtues which directly deal with the obviously hard things that may impede a man in his race to God.

There is, for example, the virtue of Christian courage, or fortitude, which equips a man to endure the extreme of danger and difficulty, even the danger of death. The Gift of the Holy Ghost, coming to the perfection of this virtue, enables a man to stride into those dangers with the confidence of God; indeed, by the gift he truly escapes those dangers, not only in the triumphant climax of divine action which gives him eternal life and the end of all dangers; but here and now the divine magic eliminates the danger and all fear of it. We have no record of the early Christian martyrs running in terror from the lions; yet often enough the lions did retreat from so tough a specimen as an early Christian to whom death was no longer a danger but an invitation to life. When the truth of history trickles out from under the iron curtain that hides the horrors of modern martyrdom from our eyes, we shall have even more abundant evidence of the work of the Gift of Fortitude than ever was furnished by the bloody persecutions of Rome. As in the early ages of the Church, so today the calm strength of divine courage is not less in the living than in the dying; a truth seen clearly enough in Eastern Europe where the living must shield the flame of the faith with their bodies. Yet is it no less clearly to be seen by the observant in the faithful of Western Europe and America where the defense of truth and morals has the apparent hopelessness of a fight against an enshrouding fog or an entwining serpent. This is an age for the Gift of Fortitude, as is any age where the world howls again for Barabbas rather than Christ and blasphemously calls down on itself the blood of God.

Magnanimity and magnificence are not blood brothers of the virtue of fortitude, for there is in them nothing of sorrow, danger, or death. They do, however, harbor a tremendous difficulty for the average Catholic, the difficulty of greatness; yet great we must be by the very fact that Christ has entered into our lives, though these seem as far apart from greatness as the humble labors of Joseph at his trade in Nazareth. It is no small thing to have the clamorings of trifles beat in waves on our ears, yet listen only to the few words of the important concerns; to continue undeviatingly to the far goal as men rush here and rush there all about us, snatching at the bright, near satisfactions; to conserve our strength for the crucial fights and then use it crushingly. This is not easy, for it requires that we be far above the surface chaos of presumption, ambition, vanity, and pettiness. It demands great depths of courage to have in our hearts the visions that produce the great cathedrals, to use money masterfully or, what amounts to the same thing, to refuse to cringe before the threat of the lack of it, to see our days and our works in terms of creative beauty worthy of our shared divine life and to labor that the realities measure up to the dreams. This is hard; particularly hard for an age that has gone stingy, stingy with money, with labor, with love, even with dreams and with life. It is vivid testimony to the work of the Holy Ghost that, in the midst of that plague of stinginess, we should come again and again upon the healthy heartiness of the great-souled, the utterly generous among the lowliest of the followers of Christ.

There is little of greatness in the material of the small sorrows where patience works, or in the steady drip of time on the rock of a man's life where perseverance keeps a man's heart from surrender.

But both of these, patience and perseverance, belong with the virtue of fortitude in their confrontation of danger and sorrow. Under the Gift of Fortitude, patience is much more than the dogged refusal to surrender to an enemy against whom we are helpless to strike a blow in retaliation for the battering we have received; for now it flows from a superb divine confidence. It is no longer a sad courage easily marking off the old from the young, but a sparkling courage that fends off the blows of sorrow, not lessening them but keeping them well away from the inner sanctum of the home of a man's heart. About it is a young alertness such as enabled the Savior to see, through the blood that covered His eyes from the crown of thorns, the future sorrow of the women of Jerusalem, the desperate need of the dying thief, the loneliness of His mother, and the awful punishment of His persecutors; to see these things, and to pity the sorrows of others. The heart does not grow old, tired, resigned, embittered under sorrow borne like this; rather it is widened, deepened, seasoned for understanding and strengthened for pity. As in the case of the dangers of death transformed by the Gift of Fortitude, so here, too, the very sorrows that patience meets, by the mysterious touch of divinity, become much more opportunities for the proof and expression of love than weights tied to a drowning heart; occasions for filling up the sufferings of Christ; apostolic weapons against the woes of the world; invitations to return the divine caress which they undoubtedly are.

Being made for eternity, we do not bear time lightly. We more easily start things or end them than bridge the gap between beginning and end; for beginnings are joyous, adventurous things, and goals are such blessed relief, whereas in between is only that deadly succession of moment after moment. The long, almost perennial delays in the advent of the good things we had hoped for, along with the thudding march of routine across the span of our days, demand the kind of courage from a man which we call perseverance. A man beaten by time is battered into effeminacy or confined within a prison of stubbornness; a man strengthened by courage is neither soft nor stubborn, but nevertheless bent under time's weight, slowed to a plodding pace, familiar with resignation and the flight of dreams. With the aid of the Gift of Fortitude, the divine impulse of the Holy Ghost, time is not merely put up with, it is confidently met with the thrust of eternity. Striding forward with the confidence of God, this man grows younger as eternity takes a greater place in his life; he knows that heaven begins with the embrace of God, and time is too short to return that divine caress. It is not softness, not stubbornness, but the resiliency of an increasing youth that marks his duel with time.

Not the least of the virtues perfected by the Gift of Fortitude is that which is one of the mainsprings of that divine violence which storms the walls of the kingdom of heaven; that stupendously strong virtue which holds in check the most violent and rebellious of all the passions, the passion of anger, and makes a powerful servant of its force instead of a usurper of peace. That virtue goes by the name of meekness. To our shame let it be said that we have inextricably bound up this name with timidity or even cowardice as if, somehow, it were a mark of strength for a man to lose control of himself under the onslaught of anger. It was not weakness in Christ that held back the twelve legions of angels who could so easily have effected His rescue and destroyed His murderers; nor is it weakness in almighty God that withholds the divine thunderbolts as the sinner hurls his puny defiance in the face of the Omnipotent. Paul was not weak, though he bowed to a Roman sword; nor was Dominic timid though he struck no blow at the attacking assassins. Control of this violent passion is a matter of strength and of courage. This is a hard thing to do. Under the Gift of Fortitude, meekness is not only in control; the rebellion of anger does not get to the stage of an uprising. Rather, in the face of injury there is a serene tranquillity which, for want of a better word, we call sweetness; a quality that wins men's hearts instead of cracking their skulls, that meets the injurious blow with a divine confidence that, more quickly than anger's recognition of injury and movement for revenge, hails the divinely commingled justice and love and throws off the blow by welcoming the caress.

St. Augustine took the beatitudes in the order in which they are enumerated and, matching them with the corresponding order of the Gifts of the Holy Ghost, found the heights and the rewards of this Gift of Fortitude in "Blessed are they that hunger and thirst after justice, for they shall be filled." St. Thomas saw some fittingness in this, for he agreed that it was very hard indeed to pursue the works of virtue with a desire that was insatiable, with the eagerness of a starving man clutching at food, or a thirsty man reaching for water. Yet, considering the matter quite aside from a framework of mere enumeration, he preferred the beatitude: "Blessed are the meek, for they shall possess the land," arguing that the high point in undisturbed tranquillity from those most violent passions of the irascible appetite is reached in the Gift of Fortitude's perfection of meekness. Still other theologians see the most fitting correspondence between the Gift of Fortitude and the beatitude of martyrs: "Blessed are they who suffer persecution for justice' sake, for theirs is the kingdom of heaven." In all three opinions, the point stressed is the superb height of Christian courage, the complete tranquillity of soul, the untroubled confidence that is no less than a participated confidence of God. In confirmation of this, St. Thomas sees the chief delight of the Gift of Fortitude in that complete and undisturbed confidence; indeed the security of the possession and enjoyment of the vision of God in heaven is nothing less than the eternally enduring reward by which the Gift of Fortitude continues past the borders of this life. A foretaste of that eternal security is had in the enjoyment of the fruits of this Gift of Fortitude in this life: the perfect disposition of man in the tranquillity of patience in the face of imminent evils, and the serene expectations of longanimity in the delayed arrival of long hoped-for goods. Security, tranquillity, solid confidence, a masterful domination of the violent surgings of irascible appetite; these are the work of the Gift of Fortitude. There is sense indeed, divine sense, in the echoing "Fear not" of the Savior.

Let us come down to particulars. Where would we expect to find the Gift of Fortitude most obviously at work in the life of the average Catholic? What are the obvious occasions for its activities? Where is it most clear that we have barred the movement of the Holy Ghost and allowed fear to conquer our souls? The general answers to these questions follow from the very nature of the Gift of Fortitude: the gift is most necessary where there is a threat to the tranquillity of the soul from lack of courage; the gift is most obviously thwarted when cowardice takes over and surrenders the fortress of our soul to the challenge of fear.

To take the negative side first, since defects of virtue, thanks to long propaganda, seem so much more quickly evident to our minds, we can readily indicate some of the surrenders of cowardice, though we have difficulty in giving an exhaustive list of these collapses of Christian courage. We attempt to hide, instead of striding confidently against the threatened evil, by such pitiful stratagems as whining, deceit, slyness, or evasion. Perhaps the contemptuous heights of this sort of cowardice are reached when we try to hide the truth of things even from our own mind: when, for example, we give murder a longer, more melodious name, the better to countenance it; or, by the same trick, find approval for polygamy, polyandry, and license in marriage; let selfish contempt parade under the trappings of love, cheating become good business, lying become diplomacy, and compromise of principles the triumph of statesmanship.

Courage has collapsed no less truly when our answer to the challenge of fear is a brutally unreasoning blow of anger, a hidden but devastating turmoil of revengeful thoughts, the continued pitilessness of unkind speech, or the rasping inconsideration of impatience. We stand paralyzed through lack of courage in all the manifestations of wavering indecisions or the hand-wringing helplessness of pettiness of soul. Habitual vice is obviously a complete surrender to the enemy, as is collapse and despair in the face of sorrow. Among other more obvious evidences of the triumph, at least to some degree, of cowardice are the flight from the labors of virtue evident in instability in good, smoldering embitterment, and plain laziness.

The triumphs of cowardice make a sorry picture, especially in an age that so patently makes demands for a courage worthy of martyrs, or even a courage beyond that of martyrs; a courage that will not only face death confidently, but will dare to walk confidently through the days, months, and years of life. The peculiar danger of this surrender to cowardice, and in a way its peculiar solace, lies in the fact that we drift slowly, almost imperceptibly, into it; we are not so perverse as to plunge deliberately into its most degrading depths. We know our reasons for confidence. We know of the omnipotence of God, His infinite love, the living Christ among us, the unwavering loyalty of Mary, and the almost incredible help of the huge family of the saints. We know, too, the virtues and gifts that God has poured into our souls, the courage He has given us as our very own, over and above the extrinsic helps that are so ready to our hands.

Our drift into cowardice in spite of these helps has some explanation in two facts. First, though we know all these things, we do not see them often enough, do not bring them out of our treasure chest of faith frequently enough to remember them vividly, cherishing them. They are not fondled by our mind and heart nearly often enough to keep our hearts bursting with gratitude, imbued with the confidence of God. Again, we are too often blind to the need of this high Christian courage in the ordinary days of our life. We are quite sure that were our faith suddenly challenged by a ruthless persecutor, we would unhesitatingly die for that faith; perhaps we would, but a steady drift into cowardice is not an encouraging preparation for martyrdom. The point, however, is that we would recognize a startling challenge as an occasion for courage. Such challenges do not enter the ordinary man's life with any frequency; yet the need for high Christian courage is a ceaseless thing in all his days.

Take, for instance, the ordinary domestic life of a Christian family. There is no reason to suspect that this family will escape threats of the weight of time, of the dullness of routine, of the sorrows, little and big, that crowd our years; despite the bond of love, living so closely together will produce occasional friction, with its attendant possibilities of impatience, unkindness, and anger's violence. This home can be made a haven of reasonable peace from which many of the fruits of love can be expected, if the virtues of patience, perseverance, and meekness are in the members of the family. If those virtues are further perfected by the Gift of Fortitude, as they are, and the family gives the Holy Ghost at least the absence of positive impediments to His divine action, then this family becomes an echo of Nazareth and a promise of heaven; a tranquil home where fear has no place at the table and each day is faced with the exhilarating confidence that has the strength and peace of God in it.

The routine social and business contacts of the ordinary Catholic give repeated occasion for the control of anger by meekness, the elimination of pettiness by magnanimity; and thus give numerous occasions for the perfect operation of these virtues under the Gift of Fortitude. In actual fact, we do stumble over this perfection of Christian courage again and again in the routine family life and social life of ordinary Catholics; what we do not do is to see this perfection as such, appreciate it, and pray unceasingly that it may increase both in ourselves and in others. We see this courage again and again in the choice of a state of life, and properly so, for this is surely a moment for high Christian courage. We are inspired by the sight of young people walking unafraid into marriage, the religious life, the priesthood, undaunted by the complete finality of these choices. We are delighted by the complete co-operation of Catholic parents who, understanding and appreciating this courage of their children, add to it a hardly less inspiring courage of their own. We are immeasurably grieved by the youngsters who turn sadly away from these hard choices, for we share in their sadness, and on both sides the sadness is justified. It is deepened by the selfish parent who fights off the departure of children as if the courage of the young were in reality an ungrateful affront to the old, who seems as horrified at the prospect of cloistered life for a daughter as of a career of prostitution, or who throws every distracting enticement available before the eyes of a son contemplating marriage or the priesthood. We are right to be sad; for here even the recurrence of the Savior's "Fear not" and all its positive implementation has been in vain.

Ours is an age for courage, it is an age for martyrs, it is an age for splendid Catholic living. Now the world looks to the mystical Christ for salvation no less than it did in the early ages of the Church, hardly less than the men of His time looked to the Son of Mary tramping the roads of Palestine. It is an age for the heights of Christian courage; and we shall see plenty of that courage; but to see, we must open our eyes to that courage that is spread through our own life and the lives of others. We must see that courage and understand again the full assuring effectiveness of those familiar divine words: "Fear not."

Fortitude

(*Summary from the* Summa)

"*Fortitude implies a certain firmness of mind . . . in doing good and in enduring evil, especially concerning goods and evils which are difficult.*

"*. . . the mind of a man is moved by the Holy Spirit so that he may attain to the end of each work begun and avoid whatever dangers may threaten. This surpasses human nature, because at times it is not in a man's power to obtain the end of his work or to avoid evils and perils, because these may overwhelm him by death. The Holy Spirit, however, accomplishes this in a man by bringing him to everlasting life, which is the end of all good actions, and freedom from all dangers. A kind of confidence is infused into the mind by the Holy Spirit, who drives out any fear of the contrary.*

"*Fortitude as a virtue perfects the mind in the endurance of all dangers of any kind, but it does not suffice to give confidence of overcoming all dangers: this belongs to the fortitude which is a Gift of the Holy Spirit.*"

—*Second of the Second Part, question one hundred thirty-nine.*

IX
Swift Victory
The Gifts for Glory

Swift Victory

"Hurry up and wait" is now a familiar call in battle. On decks, in dug-outs, or at the council tables of foreign ministers of the hot and cold wars, the same "stand-by" order is a commonplace. In a struggle for power, or at least advantageous position, not only the military but most of the populace knows the breathless tension of headlong preparations and the maddening strain of tactical restraint. For most there is a mounting temptation to plunge into any possible snare or ambush rather than to crouch, peering into darkness, looking for they know not what. Yet the waiting is just as necessary to the attack as the hurrying, since only those wise in the ways of war and of peace can command the hour and the action that leads to sure and swift victory.

For those who "take up the armor of God" (Ephes. 6, 13) in the spiritual warfare of Christian life, "Hurry up and wait" is an unspoken but well-understood order of the day. As their never-idle Charity increases from grace to grace, it gathers momentum. At first, the efforts of those new-born of God, or with a renewed awareness of their rebirth, may be erratic. They may hurry to do many spiritual things, as various devotions, penances, or practices come to their attention. As true fervor grows, however, the encircling bond of Charity draws more and more to its own quiet, calm, but intense movement. All things gradually come together for a single final drive heavenward. Yet the more Charity moves to renewed effort, the more it awakens the soul to the knowledge that the distance is infinite and that it is not "a question of him that willeth, nor of him that runneth, but of God that showeth mercy" (Rom. 9, 16). By its awareness of the all-pervading mercy of God, the Charity of devout souls is not cooled. Nor do they hurry "as if" all depended upon themselves and wait "as if" all depended upon God. In both the urgent preparations for waiting and in the waiting itself all does depend upon both God and men, or rather upon God in men, since "our sufficiency is from God" (2 Cor. 3, 5). By His grace which admits and includes the co-operation of men, God urges and enables souls to hurry up by practising the virtues that prepare for victory. By His grace which operates in men to make them docile to the promptings of the Holy Spirit, God gives the calm and the confidence for waiting until the Holy Spirit Himself gives the command at the hour and for the action that leads to sure and swift victory.

In both the hurrying and the waiting, it is the "grace of our Lord Jesus Christ, and the charity of God, and the fellowship of the Holy Spirit" (2 Cor. 13, 13) in which all Christians "live and move and are" (Acts 17, 28). Because their existence, their movement, and their life with God is as yet in the world, they cannot hope for a swift victory in terms of hours or days. Nor can they expect more than a share in their final triumph while yet they are in the midst of trials. Yet even the anticipation of everlasting peace is a greater triumph than nature could promise or provide. The world can foresee a single, sweeping solution only at the price of the abasement or even annihilation of men and their efforts. In an atomic war the solution to problems is quite simple, but there are no heroes, and an unknown scientist rather than an unknown soldier would be awarded the charred ruins of nations as his triumphant monument. In any merely materialistic or naturalistic pattern of attack, there is one or another limited victory to be gained, and likewise only one way to attain it. Men must become proficient in a specialty, and they must be prepared to dehumanize themselves to be happy with what they might attain. In the ways of God there is one final victory, but there are many ways of attaining it. By His grace souls are versatile in the ways of combat and confident of "triumph in Christ

Jesus" (2 Cor. 2, 14). With a foretaste of victory through Faith and Charity, and with an experience of the ways of the "God of peace" through His Gifts, they are able and willing to engage in the work and the waiting of a whole lifetime of spiritual combat, "to resist in the evil day and to stand in all things perfect" (Ephes. 6, 13).

Motionless attention in perfection is possible only to victorious souls in heaven. When their intellect's gaze is fixed in the vision of the Divine Essence and their will is pressed hard upon its happiness, souls stand in all things perfect. Although no creature, even the human soul of Christ, can comprehend the Infinite or love God as much as He ought to be loved, souls that see and enjoy His presence act to their full capacity at all times. There is no "at ease" during eternal rest, no falling out of line from the adoration of God. Absolute attention is required and is quite easy. No distractions can trouble souls, no fatigue overcome them. They are at rest in the peak of their activity. In such perfection the mirror-view of Faith has no place, and the will no longer has its begging hand out in Hope, since minds and hearts are filled. On the other hand, "Charity never falleth away" (1 Cor. 13, 8). It goes on the same forever, altered only in its intensity, since it now sees what before was behind a veil. Likewise, all the other good habits whose nature involves no imperfection, and which can change their conditions for acting without being lost, remain with Charity, so that the soul may have an integral perfection.

In that heavenly standing in all things perfect, the moral virtues have a place. There are no occasions of sin which would require moral virtue to resist temptation, yet there is an opportunity for the tranquil and continual practice of moral virtue. The order of reason, a renewed and imperturbable prudence as it were, dominates all the elements of heavenly life and gives to each its proper attention. Temperance moderates the soul in the midst of ineffable joys with the most profound humility; Fortitude gives even the lower appetite the strength to adhere to God for all eternity; and Justice guarantees an eternal submission. Just as the order of reason remains in the moral virtues, although the matter for merit is gone, so in the relationship of souls to the Holy Spirit, with even more reason, His Gifts perdure.

In the motionless activity of heaven, where God is "all in all" (1 Cor. 5, 28), the Gifts reach their unimpeded consummation. The bond that links them together is the same as that which unites the soul to God, Charity which never fails. Although the human deficiencies of thought and love no longer require a supplement from the Holy Spirit, the Gifts enhance the fruition of divine truth and love by making souls "in all things perfect," and like God. Understanding does not so much penetrate as possess first principles, as they are present in the Divine Mind. Knowledge judges of created causes in the new context of God's providence clearly seen. Wisdom, no longer in darkness, vividly experiences the kiss of the divine mouth, and all desires sleep, but the heart watches so that all things remain in order (cf. Cant. 1, 1; 5, 2). Counsel has the happy task of governing associations in the company of the saints, and sets the norms for the affective Gifts. Piety glories on high in Him who is above all praise. Fortitude is a feeling of divine power, and Fear is a filial reverence toward the Heavenly Father, infinitely exalted above all His saints. By all of these Gifts souls "stand in all things perfect" in a truly divine way, as "members of God's household" (Ephes. 2, 20), enjoying the perfect peace of unending triumph.

Although the victory of heaven is of another day, souls may in their measure "stand in all things perfect" even in this life. Since "he who believes in the son has eternal life" (John 3, 36), he has a beginning of eternal intimate communications when "the God of all grace, who has called us unto his eternal glory in Christ Jesus, will himself, after we have suffered a little while, perfect, strengthen, and establish us" (1 Peter 5, 10). Although, ordinarily, being established in grace in this life does not exclude the possibility of sin, it does indicate the firmness of divinely infused good habits. If nothing of human malice or weakness intervenes, these habits produce their true and undeviating effects in meriting the victory of glory. So swift and sure is that triumph, once supernatural life has begun, that the very first step seems like a conquest, "because all that is born of God overcomes the world; and this is the victory that overcomes the world, our faith" (1 John 5, 4). Even those who have not the clear vision of God that would make them eternally happy have conquered by living supernaturally, and they enjoy the fruits of victorious divine living through the Gifts even in this life. In the midst of so many things that would distract them or deprive them of their happiness they are able "to resist in the evil day, and to stand in all things perfect."

In their judgment of what makes men happy those already victorious in Faith have much in common with other men, but they present also a radical contrast. According to the opinions of men, there are three possible types of life that bring happiness: a life of pleasure, a life of activity, or a life of contemplation. Christians know quite well that they cannot rest in a life of pleasure, for they are bound "to resist in the evil day," but they are not always quite as clear about their judgment concerning activity and contemplation. They sometimes think of activity as an end in itself, or even the more meritorious way to heaven. They fail to comprehend that for all Christians the normal way of life in conformity to Christ includes both activity and contemplation, and that of the two the latter is more perfect. For each way of life, moreover, for resistance to the allurements of pleasure, for action in God, and for the contemplation of God, an unending supply of both habitual and actual grace is necessary.

The logistics of spiritual warfare have not changed fundamentally, since souls and their enemies are the same now as at the temptation of Adam or of Christ. The metaphors of St. Paul concerning a breastplate, shield, and sword are perhaps not as familiar as in his time of writing, but the underlying notion of graces for defence and attack against "the spiritual forces of wickedness on high" (Ephes. 6, 13) remains identical. The content and caliber of graces vary for different souls according to the circumstances, but the general pattern is constant. There is no age in which all the graces of God are not necessary or not available. One or another grace of virtue or of Gift may be more appropriate to the moment, but none is totally dispensable. Spiritual persons are not such specialists that they carry on one type of life to the exclusion of the other, or use one virtue or Gift without employing its correlatives. The ensemble of graces united by Charity is integral to those engaged in spiritual combat. Yet even as ultimate happiness is of many mansions, so, and especially, the intermediate triumphs of this life are varied. These victories, described by Christ Himself in the Sermon on the Mount, are the beatitudes, the general criteria of Christian life for the clergy, the religious, and the laity. They are the signs of victory and the promise of eternal happiness and peace, and for each of them there are appropriate virtues and Gifts. Some Gifts and beatitudes, therefore, are especially appropriate to enjoyment of the life of contemplation, others to the endurance of the life of action, and still others for the elimination of the life of pleasure, which is hostile to the life of grace through the Holy Spirit, since "He shall not abide when iniquity comes in" (Wisd. 1, 5).

In the life of pleasure, happiness is imagined as consisting in either of two ultimate enjoyments—an affluence of external goods, such as wealth or honor, or the full indulgence of the appetites, the desire to dominate, or the pleasure-principle. The sense-goods which occupy those dedicated to a life of pleasure are not intrinsically evil, but they become evil when taken as ultimates and preferred to greater goods. Although under the guidance of the virtues of Temperance, Fortitude, and Hope, souls can moderate and control their inclinations to sense-goods, only with the assistance of the Gifts can they know sense allurements as dull and unattractive compared to divine delights. Without hesitation, and without regret, because they know them as does the Holy Spirit Himself, they spurn what might otherwise have held them captive.

The victory of the Gifts in freeing souls from the thralldom of external goods does not imply merely the rejection of wealth pursued for its own sake. On the contrary, it means a sincere spurning of material things as a norm of happiness, however useful they may be. By the Gift of Fear, Christians are afraid neither to lose the world nor to use it to gain their salvation. Yet they never accept the bourgeois measure of worldly success as a sign of predestination, or even as a symbol of true happiness. For themselves and for their fatherland they prefer justice and charity to prosperity and power, and they hold what they have received not as their own but as the property of their heavenly Father. Just as men despise a son who would avariciously await his inheritance at the price of his father's death, Christians have the deepest reverential fear in despising the very thought of substituting the good things of their Father for their Father Himself. Theirs is rather the spirit of Job, the man of grace in prosperity and in poverty, recognizing that the Lord gives and the Lord takes away, blessed be the name of the Lord. In that recognition they, too, are blessed with the first of the beatitudes of Christ: "Blessed are the poor in spirit, for theirs is the kingdom of heaven" (Matt. 5, 3). By desiring a reign of interior and hidden happiness, they are able to conquer the first of their own unruly inclinations and to despise what a prosperity- and publicity-conscious world holds dear. They win an eternal kingdom by refusing to defend a world of crumbling castles or cartels.

Because most men continue to covet what is just beyond their reach or already within their grasp, they are willing to use any force to attain or maintain it. They have a desire to dominate, to secure their possessions, and they are prepared to be ruthless, relentless, and revengeful to gain their ends. In a subtle, but still sinful, way they glorify conflict or even competition as the ultimate norms for human conduct. Abusing laws and social responsibility, they hold title to more than their share of goods with a shameless banditry. Christian life is in contrast to all this, especially when it is divinely lived through the Gift of Fortitude. Then, souls have the strength to be restrained. Although they know that God would send them legions of angels to defend them if it were necessary, they ask for only the strength to be patient in the midst of trials. They attack what would deprive them of God, and they gladly suffer the loss of what might separate them from Him. By Fortitude over a long period of time, they can be tranquil in the midst of upheaval and strong in the patient acceptance of innumerable provocations. Their strength is meekness and their reward the most precious possession, the love of God, according to the promise of Christ: "Blessed are the meek, for they shall possess the land" (Matt. 5, 4).

For those, moreover, whose desires run far beyond their possessions or their power, there are many trials. They want honor and security, and, failing to attain it, they seek consolation in sensual delights. As compensation for what they suffer throughout life, they ask at least this solace. They move from one sensual stimulant to another with diminishing enjoyment and increasing loneliness. In their profligacy they contract a disease no science can cure, heartache. They dissipate their interest and their energy chasing after things which at best may be described as frivolous, yet they are too material-minded to enjoy anything really humorous. Only those who can know the serious significance of created things can either laugh or mourn. By the Gift of Knowledge they have the inspiration to weep over the imperfection of all passing things. They know how quickly sin follows upon the slightest concession to sensual evil, and they are inspired to make a total sacrifice of such fleeting joys for their own salvation or that of their neighbor. Voluntarily they accept pain and sorrow as the price of conformity to Christ crucified, and of hearing His words of themselves: "Blessed are they that mourn, for they shall be comforted" (Matt. 5, 5).

The comfort that comes with following the way of the Cross and of resisting in the evil day far surpasses the consolations of the life of pleasure. The Gifts of Fear, Fortitude, and Knowledge make this abundantly clear, and they rid the soul of those common obstacles to the work of the other Gifts and the winning of the rewards of all the beatitudes. These Gifts are a tactical, or task, force that prepares for the assault of heaven through the works of the active life.

While resistance to the allurements of the life of pleasure is a casting aside of things beneath spiritual goods, the occupation of the active life is a personal relationship with others seeking happiness. Christians with the deepest supernatural motives engage in the works of the active life either to pay a recognized debt or to offer a spontaneous gesture of love added to justice. Mothers and fathers caring for their children, spouses fulfilling their obligations, employers and employees, all Christians in every relationship to society or to its members, are involved in works of the active life. They are aware of their obligations to "do good to all men, but especially to those who are of the household of the faith" (Gal. 6, 10). In so doing they must be prepared to forswear something, not that they inordinately desire, but that they legitimately possess. To act without hesitance, and with the firmest will, to fulfill their obligation pressed down and flowing over, they have the inspiration of the Gift of Piety. Even in the virtue of justice men have a fixed purpose to give to others, especially to God through the virtue of religion, what is due in each case. No enticement of personal gain can subvert that virtue, no deception is admissible in its dealings. In the act of Piety, however, a willingness becomes an insatiable and ardent desire. Piety sweeps aside the human longing for a land of milk and honey, or cocktails and caviar, and completely dominates any inclination to either avarice or prodigality. The victory Piety attains, imperfectly in this life and perfectly hereafter, is an abundance of spiritual goods and guarantees, since it has title to the infinite riches of God. By attending most perfectly to the fulfillment of His will, Piety shares in all that is His and enjoys the beatitude: "Blessed are they that hunger and thirst after justice, for they shall be filled" (Matt. 5, 6).

The fullness of graces they have attained through their thirst for the fulfillment of the will of God does not puff up those so intimately united with the Holy Spirit. They recognize that they have been given evidence of divine mercy so that they may themselves show that mercy to others. As the Gift of Counsel enables them to see the opportune time and way to alleviate the miseries of others, they spontaneously act by divine instinct to help those less fortunate. In their assistance to others they are aware of a great measure of justice, since what has been given to them is, in the providence of God, for the use of themselves and others according to the needs of human life. God permits many deficiencies in the world, so that men may freely compensate for them by their merciful action. They "so speak and so act as men about to be judged by the law of liberty. For judgment is without mercy to him who has not shown mercy; but mercy triumphs over judgment" (James 2, 13). That triumph is the beatitude promised by Christ: "Blessed are the merciful, for they shall obtain mercy" (Matt. 5, 7).

In mercy and justice, Christians with the Gifts of Piety and Counsel most perfectly imitate the works of God in the world, since "all the ways of the Lord are mercy and truth" (Psalm 24, 10). Through the practice of virtue, efforts at recollection, and especially through the working of the Holy Spirit within their souls, those who seem to be overwhelmed with occupations and are continually busy with Martha-living or mother-love will find a blessed release in the beatitude promised by Christ. In a moment they may be free from concern about external works, however busy their hands may be, and they will be filled with His grace and obtain mercy from God by interior consolation. Their Piety and Counsel are a practical and implicit sharing in Wisdom, the highest of the contemplative Gifts, and briefly but forcefully they have a prelude to the glory that awaits them in heaven, and even in this world through the contemplative life.

In the contemplative life the beatitudes are not so much ends to be attained as the beginning of unending interior activity. To that beginning of eternal life, even in this world, all the acts of the active life are ordered. By those acts Christians merit heaven, whereas by the activity of the contemplative life they have heaven begun in their Faith, since "he that believeth in the Son hath life everlasting" (John 3, 36). Although a Christian mother may not nurse and care for her child with the deliberate intention of obtaining a better understanding of first principles, such an understanding is a normal consequence in her spiritual development. Who could learn better by concrete experience the relationship of the part and the whole, the dependent and the causal, bounteous love and pitiable need? There are, moreover, no legitimate ways of life for Christians which do not lead to the contemplative life. If the Holy Spirit rests upon their souls and acts within them, especially through His Gifts of Fear, Fortitude, and Knowledge, to subdue their passions and self-seeking, and His Gifts of Piety and Counsel operate to project their love outward and upward, all conformed to Christ in Charity are disposed to think and love God in as divine a manner as possible. Even in the midst of necessary human cares—although the fewer the better—they are free, since "where the Spirit of the Lord is, there is liberty" (2 Cor. 3, 17). Purified of what would obscure their vision, "they shall all be taught of God" (John 6, 45). In this divine education is a reward for previous labors, or at least a sharing in the merits of Christ, and an anticipation of eternal vision. It is true beatitude begun, for "Blessed are the pure of heart, for they shall see God" (Matt. 5, 8). Seeing God even in this life is the privilege of those whose Faith has been enlightened by the operation of the Gift of Understanding. They have the purified minds of "children of light," who with a facility unknown to the sophisticated—or even educated—separate truth from error, the substantial from the superficial. In this penetrating judgment of the Gift of Understanding is both the climax and the cause of fruitful, moral, and meritorious activity. Because they have already come a long way through their co-operation with the graces of the Holy Spirit in the virtues, souls with Understanding are enabled to look at the radical principles of all further development in the spiritual life. Just as the purification of the practice of the moral virtues prepared them for the act of Understanding, so the purity of mind and heart in Understanding disposes them for complete union with God through Wisdom.

The Wisdom of the Holy Spirit, vivified by supernatural love, "rejoices in the truth" (1 Cor. 13, 7). All truth, both natural and supernatural, is of interest to Wisdom, since it provides "the true knowledge of the things that are" (Wisd. 7, 17). Its interest, moreover, is never idle, and those led by the Holy Spirit can never be bored or listless. "For wisdom is more active than all active things; and reacheth everywhere by reason of her purity" (Wisd. 7, 24). The purity of Wisdom allows it to touch upon all things and to be contaminated by none, to treat of all subjects and to be entangled in none. Wisdom has a simplicity that shares in the knowledge of God Himself and His way of judging, since "being but one, she can do all things: and remaining in herself the same, she reneweth all things, and through nations conveyeth herself into holy souls. She maketh the friends of God" (Wisd. 7, 27). Contemplating God through Wisdom, therefore, is never without its consequences. Men cannot live in love and with love without spreading abroad its benefits. In every event and in every thing, those wise in the ways of God establish or preserve the divinely intended order, which they have seen in their enjoyment of the truth. Constantly they set one thing after another—the material after the spiritual, the individual after the common good—according to the single principle of conformity to Divine Wisdom. Nothing escapes that order in their personal and social life, and with the suavity of the Holy Spirit Himself they are able to induce that order into the lives of others. They are not arrogant in their demands; on the contrary, they are appealing in their simplicity. They rearrange the thinking of all who will give them any attention, and they revolutionize their lives, but they do nothing repugnant to the good of souls. In fact, they re-establish everywhere order and its consequent tranquillity, peace. In this peace is the blessing of those united with God in divine simplicity. Promised by Christ and provided by the Wisdom of the Holy Spirit, abundant, overflowing peace is the beatitude of those who know by experience that "Blessed are the peacemakers, for they shall be called the children of God" (Matt. 5, 9).

The peace of the children of God is seldom without challenge by those who have "loved darkness rather than the light. For their works were evil" (John 3, 19). Those who follow the prompting of the Holy Spirit cannot expect to be any better treated than their Master, who won his victories over sin, the devil, and death itself, by suffering and self-abasement. Christ foresaw this suffering for His followers, warned them, and even assured them that their happiness on earth would consist in that suffering. To the other beatitudes of joy, He added the beatitude of suffering: "Blessed are they that suffer persecution for justice' sake, for theirs is the kingdom of heaven" (Matt. 5, 10).

As a universal law, suffering in battle is the price of victory, and it cannot be otherwise in a Christian life worth the living. The precious blood flowing from the side of the Savior repeats the

Sermon on the Mount. In suffering in this life is the summation of the happiness promised by Christ. Yet that suffering is never without a deep spiritual, and even social, significance. Through it the members and the entire Mystical Body of Christ are conformed to the head. By the works of mercy Christians imitate Christ as healer and wonderworker; by the unity of their Faith and religious practices they continue His life as a teacher. In His principal role upon earth, as priest-victim in the sacrifice of the Cross, they imitate Him in their own lives, as well as in the countinuance of His sacrificial act. For justice's sake they suffer and make an oblation to the heavenly Father of their spirit of poverty, meekness, mourning, thirst for justice, mercy, purity of heart, and peacemaking—and their reward is persecution. Yet through these trials the members of the Mystical Body are enabled by the Gifts and virtues "to keep the unity of the Spirit in the bond of peace, one body and one Spirit" (Ephes. 4, 3), and by God's grace "doing the truth in charity," in all things to "grow up in him who is the head, even Christ" (Ephes. 4, 15).

Growing up in the grace and imitation of Christ by suffering rather than attacking, by being wise in the ways of God and not in those of the world, by preserving purity of mind in the presence of error and malice, by helping others when they themselves are all but helpless, by desiring justice as their brothers' keepers, by weeping over a world so self-enthralled it does not know the hour of its perfection, by being strong enough to turn a second cheek to save a soul, by being rich enough in God to be carefree in their careful stewardship, by all of these Christians triumph over human nature and conquer the world. They practice the truth in love because in them by the presence of the Holy Spirit and His Gifts has been fulfilled Christ's priestly prayer, "Sanctify them in truth" (John 17, 17).

This sanctification in truth through the sending of the Holy Spirit is the swift victory of Christian life. In the measure of hours and days those who await the fullness of His coming, as those lonesome for any loved one, may hear in their hearts a plaintive cry—"The

SWIFT VICTORY

waiting is so long." Yet in terms of an eternity merited, or even begun before the soul moves itself to act, the victory is as sudden as it is astonishing. Reassured that "the God of peace will speedily crush Satan under your feet" (Rom. 16, 20), Christians have already a victory of grace. In any "age of anxiety" the least anxious of people are those who have already won an interior victory, and in an age of uncertainty and disillusionment the most certain are those with a heavenly Advocate and earthly Comforter to teach them all things.

Even for those whose knowledge of the Gifts of the Holy Spirit is limited to the assent of Faith and the reading of theological elaborations there are many blessings and a beginning of beatitude. Each deeper thought about the Gifts of the Holy Spirit is an opportunity for self-criticism and detachment. Their presence in the souls of all who have Charity and their necessity for salvation are signs of the unfailing goodness of God in preparing souls for the combat and conquest He commands for the victory of salvation. Their very limited activity in some souls is a stimulant, not to desire to use them contrary to their nature and the will of God, but to humble souls to co-operate with the graces of the virtues, and so prepare themselves for the activity of the Holy Spirit through the Gifts. Finally, the doctrine on the Gifts of the Holy Spirit gives to souls a profound awareness of the principles of the interior life of "Christ Jesus, in whom are hid all the treasure of wisdom and knowledge" (Col. 2, 3).

The hour and the action that will bring triumph by sanctification in truth are in the command of "God who always leads us in triumph in Christ Jesus" (2 Cor. 2, 14). Even now, through the enlightenment and inspiration of the Gifts of the Holy Spirit in a living Faith, that sure and swift victory has begun, because "we all, with faces unveiled, reflecting as in a mirror the glory of the Lord, are being transformed into his very image from glory to glory, as through the Spirit of the Lord" (2 Cor. 3, 18).